The Collector's Guide To

MADE in JAPAN

Ceramics

Identification & Values

Carole Bess White

COLLECTOR BOOKS

A Division of Schroeder Publishing Co., Inc.

The current values in this book should be used only as a guide. They are not intended to set prices, which vary from one section of the country to another. Auction prices as well as dealer prices vary greatly and are affected by condition as well as demand. Neither the author nor the publisher assumes responsibility for any losses that might be incurred as a result of consulting this guide.

Searching for a Publisher?

We are always looking for knowledgeable people considered to be experts within their fields. If you feel that there is a real need for a book on your collectible subject and have a large comprehensive collection, contact Collector Books.

Photographs: Les White
Cover design: Sherry Kraus
Book design: Pamela Shumaker

On cover: (Top left) Green and orange crackle-glazed humidor, 5", $40.00-55.00. Cream and green crackle-glazed humidor, 5½", $45.00-65.00. (Bottom left) Bird flower basket, 8½", $20.00-35.00. (Top right) L to r – Yellow, blue, and green-glazed Oriental figure incense burner, 4½", Mark obliterated, $20.00-30.00. Orange, green and tan Oriental figure cigarette holder, 5", no Mark, $20.00-30.00. (Bottom right) Covered candy dish supported by a pair of dogs, $100.00-150.00.

Collector Books
P.O. Box 3009
Paducah, KY 42002-3009

⊿ Dedication ⊾

I dedicate this book to
my beloved and very patient husband, Les.
He taught me to use a computer,
and he took all the pictures. What a guy!

And he, in turn, joins me in thanking our parents,
Don and Helen Proctor and Clarence and Thelma White,
for their help and support.

⊿ Acknowledgments ⊾

I approached writing this book as a student, and I was generously helped by many experts who contributed to my education in Made in Japan:

Harvey Steele of the U.S. Customs Bureau (you may have seen him as a featured guest on *The Collectors* television show) provided invaluable information on Customs procedures, Treasury Department rulings, and shared his encyclopedic knowledge of antiques.

Neal Skibinski graciously guided me through the art styles of the past two centuries and kept me on track in relating them to ceramics styles. Michael Kolobaba shared his knowledge of art styles and proofed the manuscript twice!

Bill Naito shared not only his family history in the ceramics business but provided an "inside" overview of this fascinating industry. The advice and expertise of these kind people saved me from innumerable inaccuracies; any that remain are solely due to my imperfect understanding.

Thanks to Linda and Roger Jensen and Ron Shaffer for excellent advice on photographing pieces; to Ann Brady of Orphan Annie's/Bettie's Cupboard Antiques and Curiosities, Portland, Oregon, for help with pricing; to Colleen Bulger of Antique Alley, of Portland, Oregon, for sharing the Akiyama story; to Judy Teufel, modern-day lustre glazer; and to Sonja Johnston for telling me to quit talking and start writing.

This book is a reflection of many collections, not just my own. Thank you to all who contributed pieces to be photographed and helped with pricing: **Seven Gables Restaurant** of Olympia, Washington, **Billie Dahl**, **Jeff Gassner**, and **Sewa Singh Khalsa** let us come and photograph their collections of early Made in Japan pieces, and **Jim and Kaye Whitaker** their collection of Joséf Originals.

Members of Portland's Rain of Glass Club and many other collectors contributed pieces. They are:

Janice Ahl	Aleta Johnson	Marge Reinecke
Joyce Alexander	Carrol & Lucielle Johnson	Bernice Robertson
Shirley Bolman	Sonja Johnston	Agnes Rytkonen
Karen Bowers	Bonnie Lipsey	Judy Scott
Lizzie, John, Bill & Nancy Brewer	Mike & Sandy Miles	Sue & Bob Seymour
Don Buckingham	Sandy Millius	Sherrill's Antiques
Lea Burcham	Fern Moist	Patty & Tim Spencer
Debbie, Randy, Tara & Myra Coe	Claudia Navratil	Deb Triest
JoAnn & John Dawley	James Neal	Janice Wallace
Carrie Domitz	Laurel O'Donnell	Dewey & Ann Whited
Lois Egan	Helene Piro	Aleta Woodruff
David Flemming	Josephine Piro	Bonnie Wrozek
Jewell Gowan	Lillian Hodges	

Their generosity resulted in more pictures than the book would hold!

If you collect Made in Japan, or would like to share information, ask questions, identify "mystery" pieces, receive the Made in Japan Info Letter, or order more copies of this book, write to:

Carole Bess White
P.O. Box 819, Portland OR 97207
or fax to (503) 281-2817

Table of Contents

⚐ **The Data** ⚐

⚐ Just What Is Made In Japan? ⚐

It's not Nippon
It's not Occupied Japan
It's not Noritake

SO, WHAT IS IT?

Made in Japan is everything not marked Nippon, Noritake, or Occupied Japan that was exported from Japan for the American market. But let's narrow that definition down to what is the most interesting and collectible: Made in Japan Figural and Decorated Ceramics.

Technically, ceramics marked "Made in Japan" first were produced during the sandwich of time between the end of the Hand-Painted Nippon Era in 1921, and World War II. When the United States declared war on Japan, trade ceased. After the War, Japan ended in 1952, pieces again were marked "Made in Japan." However, there were many exceptions, which are discussed throughout the Data section of this book.

The collectible category Made in Japan (MIJ) does not include all ceramics from these periods. It excludes ware such as Imari, Satsuma, artist-made pottery and porcelain, and almost anything else "good." What's left are the cheap ceramic novelties that people of good taste thought were too trashy for words!

Made in Japan is a Cinderella story. At one time, it was the unwanted stepsister of Nippon, Noritake, and Occupied ware. But no longer! Made in Japan is one of today's hottest collectibles, with its own passions and fads.

The history of Japanese ceramic exporting is short—just over 140 years. Japan was virtually a closed country until 1853. Until then, they exported only through a Dutch trading company. Other Europeans were not allowed entry, and the Japanese did not travel abroad much. The United States sent Commodore Perry to open diplomatic and trade relations with Japan in 1853. By the 1860's, Japan was trading with the West.

The Japonisme Era: 1860's – 1890

A craze for blue and white Oriental porcelain and other Japanese art swept through Europe and America in the 1860's and 70's. Japonisme – Japanese art and ceramics – was avidly collected and imitated. These pieces, if backstamped at all, were not marked in English.

Exhibitions of prints, books, arts, and crafts in Europe and America touched off this craze. The fad continued into the twentieth century. Artists such as Toulouse-Lautrec, Degas, Cassatt, Monet, and Whistler incorporated Japanese techniques and styles in their work. Maria Longworth Nichols, founder of Rookwood Pottery, drew inspiration particularly from the Japanese works at the 1876 Philadelphia Centennial Exposition. The Japanese influence was seen in other American art pottery, and was also incorporated into Nippon ware.

Japonisme includes all Japanese ceramics produced before 1891. Japonisme is still collected today. Wares such as Kutani, Satsuma, and Arita are truly antique and are priced accordingly.

The Nippon Era: 1891 – 1921
The Art Nouveau Years

Hand Painted Nippon is really the first category of backstamped Japanese collectible ceramics. In October of 1890, America's McKinley Tariff Act required that all imported goods be marked with their country of origin. The Japanese name for their country is *Nippon*. From 1891 through 1921, most Japanese ceramics exported to America were marked "Hand-Painted Nippon" or "Nippon." They often had a company name or mon (crest) as well. During the Nippon period, some of the most exquisite ceramics ever produced were exported by Japan to America.

World War I (1914 – 1918) interrupted European ceramics manufacturing. Japan was our ally and continued to produce Nippon ware. Since competition from Europe was temporarily suspended, Nippon was even more popular in America. By 1921, the U.S. Government had decided that imports must be labeled in English. The English word *Japan* was substituted for *Nippon*. The Nippon era was over, and the MIJ era had begun.

Some "Hand Painted Nippon" marks are identical in style to "Made in Japan" marks. These are "transitional" marks—the same mark with the new wording for the country of origin. As years went by, most companies changed and updated their backstamps.

Mark #52 in the Backstamps section of this book has both "Hand Painted Nippon" and "Made in Japan" in the same mark. Although this identical backstamp was used during the Nippon Era without "Made in Japan," it was used with both country of origin names on far too many pieces to be limited to the "transitional" period. In fact, not only does it appear on several pieces in this book, it is the only one of this type to appear. This is important because collectors or dealers sometimes place a higher value on having this dual marking. If you think it's worthy of a higher price—then pay and enjoy, but keep in mind that it's not that uncommon a mark.

Nippon pieces are becoming harder to find, and prices are rising. But their beauty, variety, and value make Nippon desirable. (For more information on Nippon, see Joan Van Patten's excellent three-volume series, *The Collector's Encyclopedia of Nippon Porcelain*.)

The Noritake Era: 1921 – 1941
The Art Deco Years

The beginning of the Made in Japan era coincided with the Noritake era. The difference between Noritake and plain MIJ is more than just the backstamp of the Noritake factory. It is a whole issue of superior glaze quality and design that MIJ does not always possess, but Noritake does.

Noritake produced the "Cadillac" of Japanese export ceramic ware between World War I and II. Their largest output during those years was sets of china dishes. They were priced very reasonably for the American market. Azalea is their most hotly collected dinnerware pattern, but many other patterns were produced as well.

The most distinctive Noritake collectibles of the 1920's and 1930's were the Art Deco pieces. Vases, dishes, toilet accessories, napkin rings – everything imaginable had wonderful Art Deco decorations. Most have human, animal, or floral motifs. The quality of the glaze and workmanship is superior to *most* other MIJ ware of the period.

Noritake pieces sometimes have "twins" backstamped "Japan" or "Made in Japan," and occasionally they have another company logo on them as well. There were a few reasons for this. Other manufacturers either copied the Noritake pieces, or they obtained their blanks from the same sub-factory as Noritake. Or, they are pieces Noritake made but did not backstamp with their name. The Noritake Company was fairly consistent about backstamping its products with variations of their logo, but they did miss a few things. For instance, the three-piece smoking set in Plate 141 of this book has the Noritake stamp only on the cigarette holder; the tray is unmarked, and the match holder is marked "Japan."

As with Nippon, prices continue to rise, especially on Art Deco pieces. (Two very informative volumes on Noritake ware are Joan Van Patten's *The Collector's Encyclopedia of Noritake, First and Second Series*.)

The Occupied Japan Era: 1947 – 1952
The Evolutionary Style Years

America was starved for knickknacks after World War II, and Japan needed proven sellers for economic recovery. So, the Occupied Japan era began. During these few years, a massive amount of ceramics was produced and exported to America by Japan.

Japan was physically, spiritually, and economically devastated by the War. Some of the Japanese ceramics factories had been converted to war materiel production, and others were damaged by bombs.

The Potsdam agreement allowed the American Supreme Commander, Allied Powers (SCAP) to decide what Japan could manufacture during the Occupation (9/2/45 to 4/28/52). Japan needed industries that would rebuild their economy and let them make reparations, but that would not permit rearmament. The ceramics industry met those criteria. Recovery was slow at first, but by 1948, regular shipments of ceramics were exported from Occupied Japan to America.

Most of the output during the Occupation was marked "Occupied Japan," but actually four different markings were acceptable:
1) MADE IN OCCUPIED JAPAN
2) OCCUPIED JAPAN
3) MADE IN JAPAN
4) JAPAN

If unmarked pieces arrived in America, the importer was supposed to mark them before they left Customs. Since feelings against the Japanese ran high after the war, possibly importers tried to get away with not marking them.

Identical pieces can be found with either the Occupied mark or the MIJ mark. Some early Occupied pieces may have been made from molds that survived the war, or from new molds made according to pre-war prototypes. Thus, Art Deco "skirtholder" ladies, ladies with greyhounds, or other pieces that look like they came straight out of the thirties are marked "Occupied Japan." And, since the "Occupied" mark was not always used, these pieces were sometimes stamped "Japan" or "Made in Japan." Without proof such as catalogs or ads, it is hard to tell for sure whether MIJ pieces were made before or after World War II.

In addition to these 1930's-type pieces, most other Occupied Japan ware is made in a general sort of "popular novelty" style. (Gene Florence's five-volume series, *The Collector's Encyclopedia of Occupied Japan*, is an extensive reference source.)

The Made in Japan Era: 1921 to 41 and 1947 to the Present
Art Deco to Kitsch and Everything in Between

Popular wisdom holds that the Made in Japan era began when the Nippon era ended in 1921, but it wasn't that exact. It wasn't until later in that decade—around the time of the stock market crash—that MIJ came into its own. Some early pieces of MIJ do resemble Nippon pieces. But as the Twenties roared, styles changed, and MIJ imports grew from a trickle to a veritable flood in the 1930's. (See Appendix B.) Art Deco was predominant style, but lots of pieces were made that were not Art Deco-influenced.

Made in Japan dishes were produced for every possible occasion, from teas to dinners to waffle feeds. Individual decorations often were made only for a short time, for special orders, or in fairly small quantities. This resulted in a huge variety of patterns and colors. Finding missing pieces can be very difficult.

Novelties also were made for every possible use. There were planters, pincushions, toothbrush holders, toothpick holders, match holders, ashtrays, cigarette containers – the list goes on and on. As with dishes, the big challenge is completing sets. It is exciting to find, say, all four ashtrays in a set together – but it is rare. Usually it takes years of diligent searching to complete a set. This can be frustrating, too. We seem to find duplicates of the pieces we already have again and again, but their mates elude us. That's the fascination of the hunt!

Many of the dishes and virtually all the novelties made in Japan were earthenware, not porcelain. This includes some very fine and translucent dishes that would fool most folks. The reason is that import duties on earthenware are and were much less than on porcelain. So, to keep costs lower, most MIJ was made of earthenware. (I know, you're all screaming, "She's nuts! All the best MIJ is porcelain!" But it's often not porcelain, and I'm not nuts. There is much more information on types of clay bodies in Appendix A. If you don't want to take the time to read through it, then just keep in mind that earthenware is not always crude, brown or brick-like. It can be white-bodied, sturdy, and smooth in texture. It's just not as fine, hard or vitreous as porcelain. One Customs Bureau test for earthenware is to hold a ballpoint pen to an unglazed area. The ink should dot an earthenware piece. Another is ringing. Porcelain rings like fine crystal, while earthenware tinks or thunks.)

◄ Is Everything Marked "Japan" or "Made In Japan" Collectible? ►

Most of the older items are collectible, and for several reasons. Collectors may purchase items just for the Made in Japan backstamp, or for the look or price of the piece. Some MIJ is collectible regardless of age, because it is part of another genre (such as salt and peppers, pincushions, etc.).

Nowadays more ceramics are imported from countries other than Japan. Does this make MIJ more collectible? Yes and no. For instance, the "Nippon" backstamp probably will never be used again. Nor will "Occupied Japan." These marks therefore add value to pieces. But Japan is still Japan. They may never export ceramics at the same rate they used to, but those they do are marked with the name "Japan."

So, later and present-day MIJ is not all collectible – *yet*! However, time has a way of creating new collectibles by virtue of age or type of item. In that sense, the newer MIJ is a sleeper!

◄ Were The Japanese Imitators ►
or Innovators?

In ceramics, the Japanese are often considered to be copycats. Made in Japan ceramics are no exception. Many were copies of "better" ceramics from Bavaria, Czechoslovakia, England, Germany, Prussia, and even Japan itself, in the case of Noritake's Japanese imitators! Yet the Japanese were not the only copyists.

A look at ceramics history shows that porcelain was produced in Japan beginning in 1616. A Korean potter, Li Sanpei, discovered kaolin (the ingredient that gives porcelain its hardness and fine texture) at Arita, in Japan. Early Japanese porcelains were copied from Korean and Chinese models. Gradually, the Japanese developed their own ceramics style, with blue and white decoration and enamel colors.

This style was in turn imitated in the West. European manufacturers such as those at Meissen, Worcester, and Chantilly borrowed freely from Japanese designs.

Jump ahead to the twentieth century, and the Japanese were copying again, this time for MIJ items. Was Japan full of ceramicists with no original ideas? No! It was done at the request of designers, salesmen, and importers in America, who would tell the Japanese factories what they thought would sell well in the States. Often, it was knockoffs of "better" items that they could sell more cheaply but still offer the "look." It is not unusual to find a MIJ piece and a similar German, English, or Czech piece. Which came first? That's the intriguing question! Logic says the Japanese piece is probably the knockoff!

Styles That Influenced Made In Japan Ceramics

Made in Japan ceramics were, and still are, influenced by the prevailing styles of their day.

The Nippon years (1891-1921) spanned the end of the Victorian era, the Edwardian era, and World War I: *Ragtime to the Roaring Twenties.* Nippon styles range from heavily decorated ornate pieces to simple, almost geometric designs that presage the coming of Art Deco.

The MIJ and Noritake years (1921 – 41) included the Roaring Twenties, the Great Depression, and the beginning of World War II: *the Jazz Age to Rosie the Riveter.* Noritake and MIJ styles range from traditional to Art Nouveau-influenced pieces to Art Deco. MIJ also includes the "cute" novelty items traditionally associated with this category.

The Occupied years (1948 – 1952) were the start of the Fabulous Fifties. Later MIJ includes the psychedelic sixties, disco fever, and the country craze. Through these periods, Japanese wares developed their own distinctive characters, in which we can see traces of their stylistic influences. Studying the styles of the different periods is sort of a crash course in popular art history. Let's call it Art Fads 101.

Victorian Design, 1837–1901

Many think of Victorian as Gay Nineties and over-decorated – the red flocked wallpaper look. This was part of it, but there was much more. During Queen Victoria's reign there really was no single Victorian style. The term is a catchall for various styles of the period.

Rococo was a big part of Victorian design. Eighteenth century-type colonial ladies and gentlemen, flowers, cartouches and scrolls were part of its frothy style. It was pastel, pretty, and frivolous—overdecorated, but charming in its way, and very Nippon.

"The Last Days of Pompeii School of Design" could describe Victorian classicism. Maidens from classical antiquity, brooding ruins, garlands, swags, ribbons, and urns were favorite motifs on Nippon ware.

At the same time, other interesting styles were reflected in Japanese export ceramics:

Pre-Raphaelite Brotherhood, 1848–54

A society of English painters, the Pre-Raphaelite Brotherhood included artists such as Dante Gabriel Rossetti, Everett Millais, and Sir Edward Burne-Jones. They believed that Gothic and early Renaissance art was purer than current, mass produced, over-decorated styles. Maidens with abundant, flowing hair characterize the paintings of the Pre-Raphaelites. Their work had medieval themes, glowing colors, abstract floral designs, and languid, lanky women.

Although not ceramicists themselves, The Pre-Raphaelites were "parents" of later art styles which were important influences on Nippon and early MIJ ceramics.

The Aesthetic Movement, 1870's –1990's

Puce is not a joke! It really is a color, a sort of fuchsia, and it was a favorite of the Aesthetes. Aestheticism began as a philosophy of "Art for Art's Sake." It was a light, graceful style that was supposed to replace the Victorian tendency towards stuffiness and clutter. Its influences were taken from nature and from the Gothic period. Sunflowers, peacock feathers, and lilies were favored motifs. (The lily is a linking feature between the Pre-Raphaelites, Aestheticism, and Art Nouveau styles.) The Aesthetes were wild about Japonisme, and they avidly collected Japanese ceramics.

Arts and Crafts, 1851 – 1920's

Another revolt against bad Victorian taste was begun by William Morris in 1851. His Arts and Crafts Movement grew out of the Pre-Raphaelite Brotherhood. It was a return to medieval crafts traditions, with a subtle Japanese influence. The ideal was art for everyone made by individual craftsmen, as opposed to mass production.

British Arts and Crafts advocates were John Ruskin, Charles Rennie Mackintosh, C.F.A. Voysey, Arthur H. Mackmurdo, and Walter Crane. "Stile Liberty" was an important part of the Arts and Crafts Movement. Arthur Lasenby Liberty opened Liberty and Company in London in 1875. He began by selling Japonisme but later saw the need for a more original style. In typical Arts and Crafts fashion, he turned to the past for inspiration. He made jewelry, furniture, and household items patterned after ancient Celtic designs. Liberty sold ceramics as well, and some Nippon pieces are very similar to Liberty pieces by Moorcroft.

The American Arts and Crafts movement is seen in the Mission Style of Gustav Stickley, the Roycroft products of Elbert Hubbard, and the works of Frank Lloyd Wright. In America, it was also known as Craftsman Style. Louis Comfort Tiffany, though better known for stained glass and art glass, also produced Arts and Crafts-style pottery. Other pottery companies such as Rookwood, Weller, and Roseville were also part of the American Arts and Crafts movement. Nippon and a few very early MIJ ceramics show Arts and Crafts influences.

Art Nouveau, 1890's – 1920's

Art Nouveau's signature was the sinuous whiplash or "cigarette-smoke style" curvilinear line. Favorite themes were women with flowers in their wavy, streaming hair, and motifs from nature, such as peacocks, dragonflies, and moths. Art Nouveau was considered daringly modern for its time. The term means, literally, "new art."

Maison l'Art Nouveau, the late nineteenth century Parisian shop of Samuel Bing, gave its name to the style. Art Nouveau was a continuation of the rebellion against the fussiness of Victorian style and the blandness and bad taste of mass-produced decor. It was the European culmination of the Pre-Raphaelite, Aesthetic, and Arts and Crafts styles. In fact, much of the later Arts and Crafts output is so similar to Art Nouveau as to be indistinguishable. In Nippon ware especially, but also in early Noritake and MIJ pieces, there are Art Nouveau influences, particularly in the shapes of vases and in decorations. Art Nouveau in turn gave rise to newer traditions:

Sezession Movement, 1900 – 1920

The Sezessionists led yet another art revolt. They considered Art Nouveau excessive. The Sezession movement arose throughout Germany and Austria, as well as Russia and Japan. Avant-garde artists and craftspeople, such as those who formed the Wiener Werkstatte in Vienna, refined and simplified Art Nouveau. Heavily influenced by the works of Charles Rennie Macintosh, they created a new style. Its austerity and spare, geometric lines made it a forerunner of Art Deco.

Art Deco, 1920 – 1940's

Think of New York's Chrysler Building or Radio City Music Hall and you can envision the outline of the Art Deco style. It was simple, yet highly stylized, and based on natural and geometric forms, such as the ziggurat. In its time, it was known as Art Moderne, Jazz Pattern, or Skyscraper Modern. The term "Art Deco" actually was coined in 1966. A Paris exhibition, "Les Annees '25," featured works from the famed 1925 "L'Exposition Internationale des Arts Decoratifs et Industriels Modernes." The 1966 exhibit was nicknamed "Art Deco," and that remains the common name of the style today.

Art Deco had several influences besides the Sezessionists. Walter Gropius's Bauhaus School of Germany, founded in 1919, contributed streamlined designs and bright colors. Inspired by art such as African masks, Egyptian bas-reliefs, and the geometry of Paul Cezanne's still lifes, Pablo Picasso and Georges Braque created Cubism in 1908. Cubism in turn contributed distortion, angularity, and geometric shapes to Art Deco.

King Tutankhamen's tomb was discovered in 1922, and the resulting interest in Egyptian designs and artifacts added forms to Art Deco. Jazz music was reflected in Art Deco's brilliant colors and syncopated, repeated designs. Perhaps the best known representation of jazz in Art Deco is the American Viktor Schreckengost's famous "Jazz Bowl" punch bowl. Fashion designers and illustrators such as Erté contributed the prototype for the "skirtholder" ladies.

Art Deco ceramics were decorated in two main styles: profuse and geometric. Profuse has repeated flowers, fruits, figures, or stylized forms completely covering the piece. Geometric has a simpler, cleaner, more "machine age" look. Most Noritake and MIJ ceramics that are Art Deco fall into the latter category.

Modernist, 1950's

The fifties really were fabulous! There were cars with big tailfins, boomerang-shaped coffee tables, and Sputniks zooming on the draperies. And there was fifties Deco, some of it so thirties-like you'd swear it was from the Depression. Modernistic designs were everywhere—except on most MIJ ceramics.

Japanese export ceramics existed on the outskirts of fifties design. MIJ pieces such as chartreuse Oriental statuettes are true fifties form. But usually their style is more general, designed for the decade when mass consumption really got entrenched. High style fifties modernist ceramics were made mainly in America and Europe.

Kitsch, Beginning of Time to the Present

To sculpture, kitsch is painted cement garden gnomes. To painting, kitsch is Elvis on velvet. To ceramics, kitsch is MIJ! Kitsch is where MIJ really takes off. Kitsch is such bad taste it becomes attractive—the "ya gotta love it" school of design. Any category of MIJ ceramics you care to name also has its kitschy pieces, even if it has lovely ones as well. Take wall pockets, for instance. For every classy Art Deco floral design, there's a silly, big-billed pelican grinning at you!

Kitsch is the by-product of a consumer society. Mass production provides art and decor for every economic level and caters to all tastes. In MIJ, kitsch themes are the cute (silly animals), the sentimental (children), and the downright vulgar (toilet humor).

Later Styles

Fifties modernist was the last artist-based style to be reflected in popular, mass-produced ceramics. Later ceramics styles came from popular culture or decorating trends.

There are lots of 1950's Early American MIJ pieces, particularly salt and peppers and other kitchen items. But by the time Mediterranean furniture swept America in the 1960's, the ceramics industry had changed. Fewer pieces were being made in Japan, and knickknacks were not as popular as they once were. Few MIJ pieces were made for cultural fads such as the "psychedelic" age of the sixties and early seventies, or the Disco Era of the seventies.

The country look of today (or "duck on a stick" as one dealer calls it) and the current nostalgia craze have made knickknacks popular once again.

Mr. Hide Naito's first shop in Portland, Oregon (just to the left of Hotel Ansonia sign).

⩗ Profile of a Made in Japan Importing Company ⩘

Made in Japan ceramics importers are as interesting as Made in Japan ceramics. One of America's foremost import companies, Norcrest China, is headquartered in Portland, Oregon. Mr. Bill Naito, co-owner, was kind enough to share his family and company history:

My father, Hide Naito, emigrated from Japan to America in 1917. He opened his first gift shop in downtown Portland on S.W. Washington, the H. Naito Company. He opened a second store on S.W. Morrison and operated both stores throughout the 1920's. Then the Depression came, and in 1930 he ended up with just the Morrison Street store.

He sold mostly Oriental curios such as incense burners, god and goddess figures such as Buddha and Kwan Yin, Chinese tapestry-type runners, table mats, dishes, and Imari and Satsuma ware.

In the beginning, he did not import directly but bought from other Chinese and Japanese importers. Then about 1933 he started importing novelties, figurines, and salt and pepper shakers from Japan. These things were available before 1933, but in fairly small amounts. The thirties are when the novelty business really took off. In those days, a lot of people smoked, so he sold a lot of ashtrays!

Our building was a quarter block, with a basement where we stored rows and rows of salt and pepper shakers in boxes. Every Saturday I would go there and open the wooden cases and stock the shelves.

He had one salesman who traveled, selling to various retailers in the Pacific Northwest such as the Seaside Agate Shop. A pair of salt and pepper shakers sold for about 25 cents!

My father was not a distributor for Noritake China. Dishes were produced in Japan by sub-factories, so my father sold the same dishes as Noritake but they had different backstamps.

He also sold little Japanese flower pots with cactus plants. He would work a 50 – 60 hour week, and on the weekends he would plant cactus. He worked very hard.

One evening he came home pretty downhearted. He said "I've sold one dollar—total sale—one dollar."

But you could get a quart of milk for a nickel. I remember how I used to go to the grocery store with 10 cents, and I'd get a loaf of bread, a quart of milk, and have a penny for candy.

Then came World War II. December 7, 1941, was the beginning of the end of our peaceful life. The next morning, the U.S. Treasury Department closed my father's gift shop. They put a red sticker on our front door and locked us out. My father received permission to reopen his store, but on January 31, 1942, the Portland City Council unanimously passed an ordinance canceling all business licenses of Japanese aliens.

On February 19, President Roosevelt issued Executive Order 9066, authorizing the Western Defense Command to evacuate nearly 120,000 Japanese-Americans from the entire West Coast.

There was a window of opportunity called "Voluntary Evacuation" during which the Japanese were allowed to leave the Coast. Coming out of the Great Depression, not many could afford to get re-established, so very few were able to leave. Those who stayed were interned in camps for the duration of the War.

My family was not interned. We had relatives in Salt Lake City, so we left everything behind and went to Utah. We survived the War by raising chickens and eggs.

I wanted to join the Navy and fight the Japanese, but the Navy, Air Force, and Marines didn't allow Japanese-Americans to join. The only military service open to us at the time was Nisei, a segregated military unit. I joined that unit. It is claimed that our contribution shortened the war with Japan by two years.

It was not until the winter of 1945 that my family was allowed to return to Portland to pick up the pieces. Our shop had stayed open in Portland during the War. We were able to put the business in my brother's name. He was born in America, so he was an American citizen. Our landlord, Miss Betty Lou Roberts, never threw my father out. She continued to rent to him in spite of his being an "enemy alien."

Mrs. Saunders, who had worked for my father for about 10 years before the War, ran the store for him. She was able to buy some things, and we had that basement full of stuff. She managed to sell it even though there was so much bad feeling against the Japanese. She was not Japanese.

During the war there were a lot of newcomers here working in the shipyards and industries who didn't particularly care if things were marked Made in Japan. And, that type of novelty got quite scarce – yet people were after them because they all had jobs.

I do remember that there were comics and cartoons against the Japanese. There was one where a lady throws a plate at her husband, it crashes, and the caption says "that's fine because it was made in Japan." That's kind of cutting off your nose to spite your face because Americans had already paid for the dish! There was some of that, but many people had the common sense to know that you had to have plates, whether or not they were made in Japan.

During the War, there was a lot of California pottery being sold. Then when Dad got back after the War, say in 1947-48, we sold and wholesaled California pottery because there were no Japanese imports at that time.

We had an agent in Japan from before the War, and when the country stabilized and started production again, we started to import novelties again. These mostly had 'Made in Occupied Japan' backstamps. Then gradually we expanded more, our sales force increased, and we were importing and distributing novelty ceramics throughout America and Canada as Norcrest China Co. and Pacific Orient Company.

In 1962 we opened our first Import Plaza, kind of an import discount store. For the Seattle World's Fair in 1962, we had a Space Needle salt & pepper shaker. It took us 10 years to get rid of it! We must have produced more than 100,000. For over 30 years we have been the official licensee of Smokey Bear figurines and salt and pepper shakers and savings banks, everything made out of ceramics. Miniature bone china animals have been kind of a bread-and-butter item for us. Today, they're made in Taiwan, because the cost in Japan has risen so high. The Japanese ceramic factory workers are now making Toyota cars and VCR's and goods like that.

The Japanese have opened up factories in Taiwan, Korea, Malaysia, Mexico, and the Philippines. There was even a Noritake china factory in Sri Lanka, but I think they closed. And ceramics are being produced in China. Before the War, in the thirties, there must have been maybe a dozen companies importing Japanese ceramics; there were not very many. There was China Dry Goods of San Francisco that imported Japanese ceramics as well as giftware from China. And Quon Quon of Los Angeles.

After the War there was a very large group of importers from the East – New York, Cleveland, places like that – that got into this business and thrived. Lefton China of Chicago used to be our big competitor. Also on the West Coast are Takahashi and Otagiri, two San Francisco importers who sell nationwide.

We've absorbed Pacific Orient Company into Norcrest. We are still importing from all over the world, but mainly the Orient, the Pacific Rim countries. We have about 30 outside road salesmen, and we show at most of the trade shows in the country. We print our catalog twice a year.

There are eight Import Plaza Stores now, and we have 13 Made in Oregon Stores. It's unusual for a business to last for more than 70 years, but we've done it.

Manufacture Of MIJ Pieces

Most Made in Japan novelties are made from liquid clay (called slip), usually a white-bodied, but occasionally reddish brown, earthenware. The slip is poured into a mold. When it dries a bit, the piece is removed from the mold and partially fired in a kiln, so that it is still porous. At this stage, the piece is called a blank. Then it is glazed.

The colors on a piece are glazes. If you turn over a piece of MIJ, all or part of the bottom is chalky white, or occasionally reddish brown. This is the unglazed foot of the piece, the actual clay body. The foot is left unglazed because, if glazed, it would fuse to the kiln shelf.

Glaze is made from powdered minerals mixed with water, and it is either painted or sprayed on, or the piece is dipped in it. The piece is then re-fired, and the glaze hardens to a glass-like coating.

MIJ pieces have five basic types of glaze:

Lustre

Lustre is probably the most popular glaze on MIJ pieces. It is made from metallic salts applied in a thin layer to a piece that already has a base glaze of clear or white, then re-fired. Because lustre salts are delicate, they are fired at much lower temperatures and are not as strongly bonded to the piece as the base glaze. This is why lustres can be damaged—they are thin and soft and can be rubbed off or scratched. The lustres on dinnerware usually are sturdier than on novelties, so they won't mar as easily. But they still need gentle treatment.

Tan and blue are the most common lustres, but there are also shades of cream, green, ivory, orange, white, yellow, and rarely, pink and lavender. Gold and silver are also lustre colors, and they are used sparingly as accents on a few of the older MIJ pieces. Black is the more common color for accents and outlining on older MIJ pieces.

Bisque

Bisque is really a lack of glaze, rather than a glaze type. Bisque pieces are not covered with a base glaze, so they are not shiny, and you can feel the texture of the clay body. They are sometimes colored with stains or paints, and they often have some glazed areas.

Crackle

Crackle is the web-like network of fine lines in some glazes. It results from the body and glaze cooling at different rates. Sometimes stain is rubbed over the piece to accentuate the crackle.

Matte

True matte glaze is entirely opaque with no shine at all. Most MIJ pieces that are matte-glazed do have a little reflection, but not enough to be called shiny.

Shiny

Shiny glazes have a glossy surface that reflects light. Sometimes they are called bright or gloss glazes as well.

Two identical pieces are sometimes different sizes. If they are fairly close, it is probably due to firing temperature (the hotter the temperature, the smaller the piece), or differences in the clay bodies. If there is a greater difference, say 25% or so, it may be because a mold was cast right from an already fired piece. As the mold dried, it shrank, so the pieces cast from it would be smaller than the original. If there is a really big difference, it is probably because the Japanese sometimes made "mini" versions of pieces.

Dating Made In Japan Pieces

Those three little words, "Made in Japan," may or may not determine the age of a piece. Lots of collectors believe that the backstamp "Made in Japan" means a piece is pre-World War II, and the backstamp "Japan" means it is post-Occupation. And an equal number of collectors believe exactly the opposite! Collectors want absolutes, and there aren't many in dating Made in Japan pieces. Why? Because of Customs regulations and World War II.

According to Mr. Harvey Steele, former Antique Specialist and currently Field National Import Specialist for the U.S. Customs Bureau in Portland, Oregon, the change in backstamps from 'Nippon' to 'Japan' to 'Made in Japan' occurred slowly and not uniformly:

There was one basic marking law, the McKinley Tariff in 1890. The wording was changed under the Tariff Acts of 1909, 1922 and 1930, but really not a lot.

In addition to these Tariff Acts, which are the Law of Congress, there is a large body of administrative law. Some of that is Treasury Decisions or Abstracts, and those are available to the public in book form for every year back to the last century.

Unfortunately, a lot of administrative law is no longer available. There are internal bureau letters and rulings that were not published as Treasury Decisions, which we discarded as they became obsolete. In the first 20 years of the twentieth Century, a lot of wares were marked either 'Nippon' or 'Japan.' Even before 1921 some were marked just 'Japan.' The usual marking at that time was a printed backstamp with 'Nippon' or 'Japan.'

I remember seeing a report from an Appraisers Conference, possibly from 1914, that instructed Inspectors that the words *Made In* should appear with the country of origin on imported goods. But I no longer have the document.

The laws and rulings were not enforced uniformly. There were local options, and Import Specialists and Appraisers interpreted the laws differently. So items imported through Los Angeles might be stamped differently than items imported through Portland.

Before World War II, Customs had guidelines for the use of the telephone. Typically, only the Collector and the Chief of the Outside Division had phones, and most calls were local. The idea that they would get on the line to the New York Specialist about interpreting these laws just didn't happen. That was done by "snail mail," by correspondence, and it was invariably a very slow and tedious process.

Many antique specialists consider it a general rule that before 1921 items were not marked "Made In." In fact, before 1921 most countries marked their items just with the country of origin name—just "Germany," "England," etc. In 1921, for a variety of reasons, a lot of countries began marking their goods "Made In."

There were many companies that had "Nippon" in their names. Nippon Toki Kabushiki Kaisha [the parent company of Noritake] was by far the biggest, but there were many others.

This mark [#52] says "Hand Painted Nippon, Made in Japan." I'm sure by the looks of it that it is from the 1930's, and the name of the company is one of the many Nippon companies.

A watershed marking decision was an Abstract made under the 1930 Tariff Act prohibiting loose, pasted labels. If the label were pasted on in an extremely firm manner, we granted a waiver to this. But most came off too easily, so the usual marking was a printed backstamp on 1920's and 30's pieces.

In the 1950's, if a shipment came in with no mark, or with small paper labels that came right off, we would give them 30 days to mark it. There were companies in America that specialized in printing embossed metallic paper labels that could be affixed with very strong glue. They were very shiny.

I was in Japan during the Occupied period. We saw new items that were indistinguishable from those of the 1930's. But there was also a great eclecticism during the fifties and sixties. They were trying to find styles that would match the period. There wasn't any definite style, and they were searching for styles.

So, we know from Mr. Steele that the majority of pre-World War II pieces are marked "Made in Japan." But this wording is not a *guarantee* of age, because there were plenty of pieces from both before and after 1921 that just say "Japan." We also know that the words "Made In" were not required by law (American or Japanese) on backstamps at any time, but that the Customs Bureau directed that they be used. And even at that, they were not always used.

Also, we know that prior to the change in law, "Nippon" was an **acceptable** marking, not **required** one, so pieces could be marked either way. After the new ruling was published March 1, 1921, there was a grace period of six months, so "Nippon" was still acceptable until September 1, 1921. Too, the law did not require backstamp inks to be certain colors, just that they be indelible. So if you have heard, for instance, that a red "Made in Japan" mark means a piece is older than one with a blue "Japan" mark, or *vice versa*, forget it!

Pieces in a set were marked either "Japan" or "Made in Japan," depending on how much room there was for marking. Really small pieces in a set often were unmarked as long as the larger pieces were marked.

Some pieces also had company names or mons (crests, or logos, as we would call such symbols today); others did not. Some were marked "Hand Painted" as well; most were not.

Pieces made from 1947 through today are either marked "Made in Japan" or "Japan" (or "Occupied Japan" or "Made in Occupied Japan" if they were made from 1947 to 1952.) Ceramics sold in Japan to Americans for personal use did not have to be marked at all. Other countries had marking rules that were different from ours, or they had none at all. Some countries required imported goods to be backstamped only with the word *foreign*. (See plate 74.) So, pieces brought to America from other countries for personal use, not for sale, may have the word *foreign*, or no marking.

Finally, compliance with our laws was not consistent. U.S. Treasury Decisions and Tariff Acts clearly required that pieces be marked with both the country of origin and the name of the maker or purchaser (T.D.34740). The latter rarely happened. Very few of the older pieces have the company name of the seller on them. (One line that does, for example, is Lefton China.)

According to Howard Kottler, the late, eminent Noritake collector, there were about three large and thousands of medium to small producers of ceramics in Japan before World War II. Unlike large factories such as Noritake, the individual family kilns and small ceramics companies did not have backstamping systems for their own records, so marking was apt to be done in a haphazard fashion, if at all.

The Customs Bureau tries to examine at least 10% of everything that comes into the country, but that leaves a lot of merchandise that they simply do not have the manpower to inspect. Since the small producers might or might not mark, shipments did get through Customs without the proper backstamping. Backstamps are *guides*, not *guarantees* of age.

In the normal course of things, pieces could be dated by styles even if their backstamps are unreliable. But World War II caused an unnatural hiatus in production. Styles that were becoming obsolete by 1941 were re-made after the War, so you can never be 100% certain that a piece is pre- or post- WW II unless you know its individual history.

In the 1930's, feelings against the Japanese ran high because of their invasion of China, and because any success they had in business and farming in the United States was felt by some Americans to be an encroachment. After the bombing of Pearl Harbor, there was even more anti-Japanese sentiment. And up until the electronics and automotive revolutions that changed our thinking, goods from Japan were perceived by Americans to be of very low quality. This is why marks on Made in Japan pieces sometimes have been removed or painted over.

Given all this information, if infallibly dating Japanese pieces is the most important thing to you, then you're in for some serious headaches! Documentation helps. So do personal anecdotes. Even though you can't be sure a piece wasn't re-made after the war, if you find it in a pre-War publication you at least know when it was originally made. Or, you could try "movie spotting"—looking for pieces in 1930's movies. The American Movie Classics channel is great for this.

The Tariff Acts and Treasury Decisions which affected the marking of all goods exported to the United States are in the back of this book, Appendix C.

How to Tell Old From New Pieces

First, memorize this book! Seriously, first check the backstamps. Most pieces that have "Japan" or "Made in Japan" backstamps, not labels, that *look* old *are* old. (By old I mean pre-World War II, and by new post-1952.) How will you know if they look old? By experience and study. Old ceramics are distinctive-looking, and often they aren't something commonly used now, such as figural toothbrush holders. Also, newer pieces generally do not have applied parts, such as the bird on the wall pocket in Plate 343b.

Check the bottoms for wear and dirt. Most will have some grayish, blackish or brownish discoloration. This "patina" is a sign of old age. Most newer ceramics are lighter in weight, and they have an airy, "blown" feel to them. The older ones are usually heavier and thicker.

Look at the glazes. Before WW II especially, there were not as many different colors, but pieces usually were painted with several of them. There are many more shades of color available today, but fewer are used per piece to save money. On older ceramics true red was rarely used, and orange was very common. Red is common on new imported ceramics, and they have lots more pastels, and all the colors reflect today's tastes and fashions.

Lustre glazing is another good clue. Nowadays, lustres are rare. The few there are usually are more iridescent than the older ones. Often the new lustres are mottled with a contrasting color (such as opal with mauve mottles), and have small gold or silver accents. Old lustre glazes usually were a deep, rich, solid color. Mottling was rare.

Finally, know what's being made today. Visit retail stores, or attend one of the gift trade shows held in most states every year. Look at your local ceramics greenware shop. Lots of old-looking things are made or glazed by hobbyists. At a recent crafts show, there were ceramic shoes made by casting molds of old MIJ pieces. One will probably turn up at a flea market priced as "old." New pieces are attractive, and many will be tomorrow's collectibles. But do your homework! Don't pay an "antique" price for something you could buy retail today at a five-and-dime or crafts sale.

Pricing Made In Japan Collectibles

The price of any object is established by the buyer and seller—in other words, whatever the market will bear. Prices vary by region, and they can be much higher in larger urban areas such as New York and Los Angeles. Specialties are priced higher by their experts; i.e., Art Deco pieces may be priced higher by an Art Deco dealer. Here are some guidelines to help determine the value of Made in Japan collectibles:

Condition

The bad news is that MIJ collectibles are not always found in "mint" condition. The good news is that prices reflect this, and they are still affordable!

Dishes—any items meant for food—are pretty sturdy. Watch for worn areas, scratches, cracks, and chips, which reduce the value of dishes by 50-90%. Broken dishes are worth even less. Breakage and missing parts (such as cup handles) reduce the value by 98%. Unless you desperately need them for a specific purpose, pass on them. They will not enhance your collection.

The novelties ae a different story. These items were NOT fated to survive in "mint" condition! They were mass produced for cheap, quick consumption and often were not respected or cared for by their owners. Novelties are bright, colorful, and appealing to children. Many novelties intended for adult use probably ended up in children's toy boxes. Also, lots of pieces have dirt ingrained in them. This means they were used for planters whether they were made for that purpose or not. The dirt or water/lime deposits now may be permanent. With of all this against them, it's a wonder that any novelties survived intact at all.

MIJ was decorated quickly with a slapdash flair that added to its charm but did not necessarily mean precise designs beautifully rendered. The better and more imaginative the glaze, the higher the price. While the clay bodies were fairly strong, the glazes were not the finest, and glaze flaking is common. Flaking reduces the value.

If the glazed area is smooth, and the flake is the color of the clay body, it occurred at the factory. The piece was fired after the flake, but the glaze did not melt over the area. If the glaze is rough or there is a crater, the flake happened after firing.

Check to make sure the piece has not been varnished over or subjected to other "repairs." A factory flaw is still a flaw, but amateur repairs make any piece worse.

Mint Condition

Mint condition means a state of perfection in which flaws simply do not exist:

1) Pieces are as perfect as a newly minted coin. The features are sharp and precise, with clearly defined details.
2) There are no glaze flakes.
3) There are no glaze flaws—lumps, runs, pits or fading.
4) The glaze brushwork is perfect, with no sloppy overlaps, crooked lines, or missed areas. There is no glaze crazing.
5) There is no visible, permanent dirt, lime or water damage.
6) There are no cracks, chips or damage in the clay bodies.

Excellent Condition

Excellent condition means nearly but not quite mint:

1) The details are sharp.
2) There may be tiny glaze flakes, but no more than one or two at most. They are very small, and not obnoxious or too obvious.
3) There may be glaze flaws, but, again, only a couple of small ones that aren't too bothersome.
4) There may be minor glaze crazing or small glaze brushwork errors. These add to the charm of the piece, and do not affect the value.
5) There is no visible or irremovable dirt or stains, and no lime or water damage.
6) There are no cracks, chips, or broken areas in the clay bodies.

Items in excellent condition should be about 75% of mint value.

Good Condition

Good means exactly that—not great, but not too bad:

1) The details may not be really sharp, but outlines are still discernable.
2) There may be more glaze flakes, flaws, crazing and brushwork errors.
3) There may be some visible ingrained dirt and minor lime or water damage, but no major stains.
4) There are no cracks, chips, or broken areas in the clay bodies.

Items in good condition should be about 60% of mint value.

Poor Condition

Poor condition means inferior quality:

1) The molds were worn out, so details are blurred or missing entirely.
2) There may be several glaze flakes, flaws, or brushwork errors, and they are larger and more obvious.
3) There may be chips in the clay bodies and/or cracks, whether hairline or major.
4) There may be severe water or lime damage, or gross, irremovable visible dirt or stains.
5) There may be glaze crazing or pitting, or major brushwork errors.
6) There may be hairline cracks and chips, but there are no broken areas.

Items in poor condition are 25% of the value of mint condition.

Damaged Condition
Damaged condition means that pieces have been broken in some way:

1) Pieces have been broken and glued back together.
2) Body parts, knobs, or finials are missing. Look especially for missing body parts on the novelties. I have seen figural novelties with missing hands, arms, legs, noses, etc., priced as if they were absolutely mint.

I would not give 50 cents for damaged pieces.

Repairs
Usually, damaged MIJ pieces are not valuable enough to have been sent to a professional china repair service, so they have been fixed by amateurs. If you can't live without the piece, keep in mind that it's better to have an honest chip than a badly botched repair.

Look for:

1) Chips covered with paint, nail polish, or varnish of some sort.
2) Missing parts re-sculpted with unfired clay or paste and re-painted.
3) Parts or entire bodies broken apart and glued back together again.

Boxes
Many MIJ novelties came boxed in sets. The older boxes were of lightweight cardboard, usually covered with patterned tissue paper. Boxes in good original condition add 10% to the value of the set. In damaged condition they add nothing, although they are still useful and desirable.

For box repairs that are cosmetic only, try "O Glue," a product used by sheet music collectors. It will glue the patterned paper back into place and seal tears and frays without staining. Rubber or household cement, paste, or other glues could discolor the cardboard. This type of repair is for looks only! The box still may not be strong enough to bear the weight of the pieces.

Comparative Values
Made in Japan quality and workmanship simply is not as high as that of its richer cousins Nippon and Noritake. So, MIJ prices generally will not be as high as theirs except on very rare and special pieces. MIJ is often better in quality than Occupied Japan. Prices on similar MIJ and Occupied pieces can be fairly close. However, their backstamp rather than their quality and workmanship puts Occupied collectibles in their own category and makes them more valuable. That's great for the MIJ collector who may find the same item without the "Occupied" stamp at a lower price!

Rarity
There are so many areas of collecting in Made in Japan, and each one has its rarities. Rare pieces will always cost more, unless you get lucky!

⚐ Care and Cleaning ⚐

Made in Japan glazes are not the sturdiest, so be careful when cleaning your pieces. The better-made dishes will withstand normal washing, but never put them in the dishwasher. And never use harsh or abrasive cleansers. Lustre glaze is fragile and can be rubbed off, especially on the novelties. If you find a piece with white cloudy areas in the lustre, it is because it received too energetic a washing. Sometimes you have to choose between keeping the glaze intact or having a squeaky clean piece.

Helpful Hint

Mr. Sewa Singh Khalsa, a fellow collector, shared this tip: use small balls of dental wax (available from dental supply houses) to affix pieces to shelves, or to fasten on lids. It is very strong, but it will leave your glazes intact because all you have to do is warm it with your fingers to soften and remove it.

✎ The Collectibles ✎

In the captions, pieces are listed from left to right. The labeling of pieces (pincushions, match holders, etc.), is based on research and direct knowledge, or comparison with similar objects. Keep in mind that factories would make—and sellers would market—any object for any function they thought consumers would buy. So, the same piece could have been sold as more than one thing, or the mold may have been altered to give the piece another use. (If you know for sure that a function is different from what is listed, write me!) Backstamps are referred to by number. Even though the color of the ink on the backstamps is not an indication of age, it is included anyway, where possible.

All measurements are for height, unless otherwise indicated. Measurements have been rounded off to the nearest quarter-inch. For instance, the caption for the first item in plate #1 reads "3½", Blue Mark #1 and Blind Mark #1." This means the piece is approximately 3½" tall and has a double backstamp: Black Made in Japan plus Blind (incised) Made in Japan. Sometimes the double backstamps are not the same.

Blanks were sometimes decorated by different companies, and often pieces in the same set have different backstamps or different colors of ink. So, if you have a piece that has a different backstamp from the one in the picture, that's probably the reason.

Some items are noted as Akiyama pieces. The Akiyama family had Oriental gift stores in Portland, Oregon, from the 1920's until 1942, when they were interned. They packed up their remaining stock and stored it in the dirt basement of their house. It remained there until 1987 when Hanji Akiyama, the son, sold the house, cleaned up the pieces, and placed them in a local antique mall.

Other pieces are noted "shown in the Sears catalog." This is, of course, the Sears & Roebuck catalog. A fortunate few pieces had their date of purchase inscribed on them, and others had been in their owners' family before World War II; these are noted also. Also noted are MIJ pieces that have Occupied Japan versions. Probably there are more in existence. A fun collection would be "twins"—identical pieces with MIJ and Occupied backstamps.

The following marks are backstamped, incised, embossed (raised), or labeled. Incised or embossed markings that are the same color as the background are called "blind." These are **all** the marks found on pieces in this book. There may be other marks out there. There definitely are more brand name labels, but they are on newer pieces, which are not what this book concentrates on.

There are some unmarked pieces included. Because of their "look" and "feel," their owners believe that they they are MIJ. There were so many unmarked pieces made that not to show at least a few would not truly reflect the scope of Made in Japan. A few Noritake, Occupied Japan, Nippon and German pieces are also included for the sake of price, quality and prototype comparison.

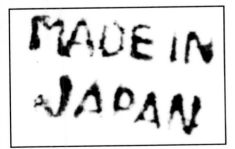

Mark 1

Mark #1. This mark is found most often on pieces in this book. Sometimes it is a different shape from the one pictured—all on one line, arranged in a circle or oval, in a different typeface—but these are minor differences and are not noted.

Mark 2

Mark 3

Mark 4

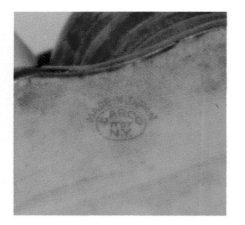

Mark 5

Mark 6

Mark 7

Mark 8

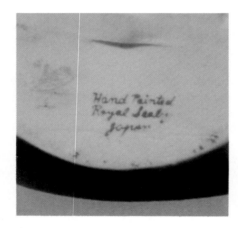

Mark 9

Mark 10

Mark 11

Mark 12

Mark 13

Mark 14

Mark 15

Mark 16

Mark 17

Mark 18

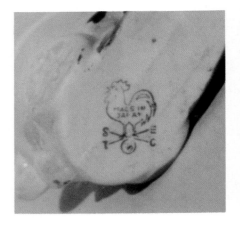

Mark 19

Mark 20

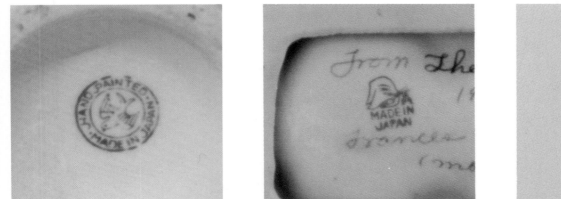

Mark 21

Mark 21A

Mark 22

Mark 23

Mark 24

Mark 25

Mark 26

Mark 27

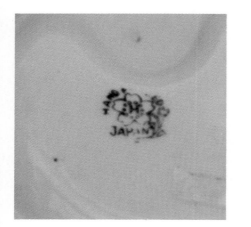

Mark 28. Top line says Hand Painted.

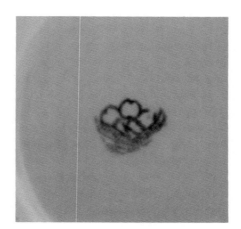

Mark 29

Mark 30

Mark 31

Mark 32

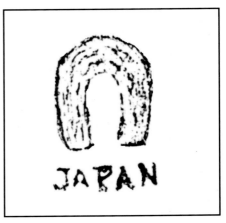

Mark 33

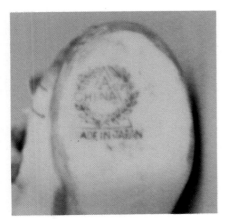

Mark 34

Mark 35

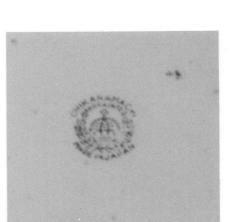

Mark 36

Mark 37

Mark 38

Mark 39

Mark 40

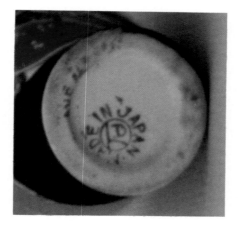

Mark 41

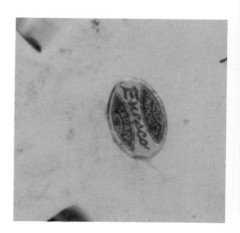

Mark 42

Mark 43

Mark 43A

Mark 44

Mark 45

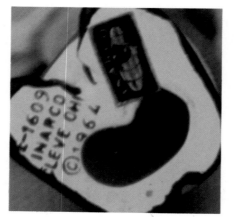

Mark 46

Mark 47

Mark 48

Mark 49

Mark 50

Mark 51

Mark 52

Mark 53

Mark 54

Mark 55

Mark 56

Mark 57

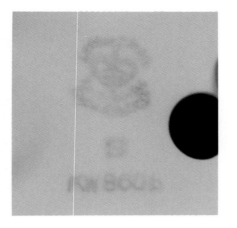

Mark 58

Mark 59

Mark 60

Mark 61

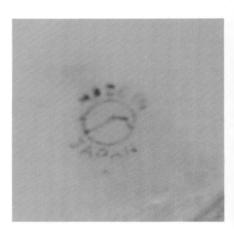

Mark 62

Mark 63

Mark 64

Mark 65

Mark 66

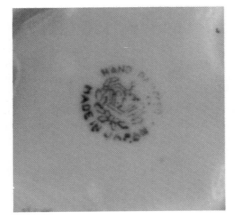

Mark 67

Mark 68

Mark 69

Mark 70

Mark 71

Mark 72

Figural Pincushions

Pincushions are fun to collect because they are among the more plentiful items imported from Japan. Because they were essentially useless, lots of them survived. However, pincushions are the perfect example of misuse. Many of them have serious dirt and lime damage inside because they were used as vases or planters. Why is it that, if something had an opening, someone felt compelled to pop a plant in it?

Pincushions—and all the novelties—have both animal and human figures on them. The humans are fairly recognizable, but often the animals are barely recognizable! These are referred to as mystery animals in the captions. (If you know for sure what any of these mysteries are, write me!)

The old pincushions almost always had velveteen or silk cushions wrapped around many different substances including newspaper, tissue paper, wood chips, straw, or whatever else was handy. Usually the newspaper was Japanese. If you could translate it, that would be another way to date your piece.

Plate 1. (a) Very rare banjo player pincushion in multi-colored matte glazes, 3½", Blue Mark #1 and Blind Mark #1, $52.00-62.00. (b) Rare blue, tan and white lustre flat-planed man pincushion, 3", Black Mark #1 and Blind Mark #1, $42.00-52.00.

Plate 2. Rare bisque sailor boy pincushion, 3¼", Blind Mark #1, $25.00-35.00.

Plate 3. (a) Boy with bow pincushion in orange, blue and white matte glazes, 3", Black Mark #1, $30.00-40.00. (b) Little devil pincushion in green lustre, 2½", Blind Mark #1, $25.00-35.00. (c) Teacher with book and cane pincushion in tan lustre and multicolored shiny glazes, 2¾", Black Mark #65, $25.00-30.00.

Plate 4. (a & c) Pair of girls with big hats pincushions in orange and black matte glazes, 4¼", Black Mark #1, $30.00-40.00 each. (b) Clown in tub pincushion in blue and white lustre, 3", Blind Mark #1, $30.00-40.00.

Plate 5. (a) Girl with big basket pincushion in multicolored shiny glazes, 3¾", Red Mark #18, $20.00-30.00. (b) Rare tall lady with basket pincushion in multicolored shiny glazes, 5¾", Black Mark #1, $30.00-40.00. (c) Lady with flowers and cat pincushion in multicolored shiny glazes, 3½", Black Mark #2, $10.00-20.00.

Plate 6. (a) Boy with mandolin pincushion or tiny vase in multicolored shiny glazes (also made with the Occupied Japan backstamp), 2¾", Black Mark #1, $6.00-12.00. (b) Man with accordion pincushion in tan lustre with multicolored shiny glazes, 3¾", Black Mark #1 and Blind Mark #1, $20.00-25.00. (c) Man with violin pincushion in yellow lustre and multicolored shiny glazes, 3", Black Mark #1 and Blind Mark #38, $12.00-20.00.

Plate 7. (a) Sailor pincushion in multicolored shiny glazes, handwritten on bottom "From Deloris Unruh, Dec. 4, 1939," 3¾", Red Mark #1 and Blind Mark #2, $30.00-40.00 (b) Matching sailor salt & pepper, 3", Red Mark #2, $12.00-22.00.

Plate 8. (a) Rare radio dog pincushion in yellow and tan lustres, a special piece because it's also desired by radio collectors, 3", Black Mark #1 and Blind Mark #1, $30.00-40.00. (b) Dog with book pincushion in multicolored shiny glazes, 2¾", Black Mark #1 and Blind Mark #2, $25.00-35.00.

Plate 9. Top hat dog pincushions. (a) Yellow lustre with black and orange shiny glaze, 4", Black Mark #38 and Blind Mark #38, $25.00-35.00. (b) White lustre with orange shiny glaze, 3¾", Black Mark #1, $25.00-35.00. (c) Tan lustre with black and orange shiny glaze, 3¾", Red Mark #65, $25.00-35.00.

Plate 10. Calico dog with lustre top hat pincushions. (a) 3¾", Black Mark #1, $28.00-38.00. (b) 2½", Black Mark #38, $25.00-35.00. (c) 2½", Black Mark #1, $18.00-28.00. (d) 4¼", Black Mark #1, $28.00-38.00.

Plate 11. (a) Carriage and pair pincushion in multicolored lustre, 1¾", Black Mark #1 and Blind Mark #1, $18.00-28.00. (b) Horse and carriage pincushion in tan lustre and multicolored shiny glazes with attached pin tray, 2¾", Black Mark #38, $18.00-28.00.

Plate 12. (a) Dog cart pincushion in blue, tan, and yellow lustres, 3¼", Black Mark #1, $25.00-35.00. (b) Calico dog and tan lustre cart pincushion, 3¼", handwritten on bottom "Frances Long (Moses Sch.), From Thelma Claycon, 1932," Red Mark #21, $25.00-35.00.

Plate 13. (a) Ox and cart pincushion in blue and yellow lustres, 2½", Black Mark #38, $18.00-28.00. (b) Rare spaniel with basket pincushion in green and yellow lustres, a major piece at 4" tall, Red Mark #1, $30.00-40.00. (c) Calico horse and yellow lustre cart pincushion, 3", Red Mark #1, $25.00-35.00.

Plate 14. (a) Bird with mushrooms in multicolored matte glazes, 3¾", Blind Mark #1, $18.00-28.00. (b) Blue and yellow matte-glazed pelican (It was sold to me as a pincushion, but it really looks like a tool to get the meat out of crab claws!), 2½", Black Mark #1, $18.00-28.00. (c) Brown and maroon shiny-glazed bird with flower pincushion, 3½", Black Mark #1, $18.00-28.00.

Plate 15. (a) Penguin pincushion in blue and white lustres, 3", Black Mark #1 and Blind Mark #2, $18.00-28.00. (b) Yellow lustre cockatiel pincushion, 2¾", Black Mark #1, $18.00-28.00. (c) Baby chick pincushion in tan lustre and multicolored shiny glazes, 2½", Red Mark #1, $18.00-28.00.

Plate 16. (a) White shiny-glazed elephant pincushion (post-1960), 2¼", no Mark, $7.00-10.00. (b) Monkey pincushion in multicolored matte glazes, 2¼", Black Mark #1, $18.00-28.00. (c) Brown and white shiny-glazed dog in car pincushion, 2½", Red Mark #2, $18.00-28.00. (d) Dog with ball pincushion in multicolored shiny glazes, 2¾", Black Mark #2 and Blind Mark #2, $18.00-28.00.

Plate 17. Art Deco animal pincushions. (a) Tan lustre cat, 4", Red Mark #1, $18.00-28.00. (b) Tan lustre cat, 3¾", Black Mark #1, $18.00-28.00. (c) Yellow lustre dog, 2½", Red Mark #1, $18.00-28.00. (d) Yellow lustre dog, 2¼", Black Mark #1, $18.00-28.00.

Plate 18. Art Deco animal pincushions. (a) Tan lustre lion, 2½", Red Mark #1, $18.00-28.00. (b) Tan lustre lion, 2¼", Red Mark #1, $18.00-28.00. (c) Blue lustre elephant, 2¾", Black Mark #1, $18.00-28.00. (d) Blue lustre elephant, 2½", Red Mark #1, $18.00-28.00.

Plate 19. Art Deco animal pincushions. (a) Tan lustre lion with blue diamond-shaped hole, 2½", Red Mark #1, $18.00-28.00. (b) Tan lustre dog (facing opposite direction of dogs in Plate 17), 2½", Red Mark #1, $18.00-28.00.

Plate 20. Art Deco animal pincushions. (a) Blue lustre rocking horse and rider, 3½", Blind Mark #1, $18.00-28.00. (b) Tan lustre elephant 3", Red Mark #1, $18.00-28.00.

Plate 21. Art Deco animal pincushions. (a) Yellow lustre cat and mouse, 2¾", Red Mark #1, $18.00-28.00. (b) Tan lustre pelican, 2¼", Black Mark #1, $18.00-28.00.

Plate 22. Yellow lustre animal pincushions. (a) Mystery animal, 2½", Black Mark #18, $18.00-28.00. (b) Dog, inscribed "Newport, Ore." no Mark, $18.00-28.00. (c) Lion, 2¼", Black Mark #1, $18.00-28.00. (d) Another mystery animal, 2½", with price sticker inscribed "Olds Wortman & King 3¢." This store was listed in the Portland, Oregon telephone directory through 1947. Red Mark #1, $18.00-28.00.

Plate 23. (a) Dog pincushion in tan lustre, 1¾", no Mark, $18.00-28.00. (b) Cat pincushion in tan lustre (pictured in the 1927 Sears catalog for 25¢), 2", no Mark, $18.00-28.00. (c) Blue lustre dog pincushion, 2¼", Black Mark #1, $18.00-28.00.

Plate 24. (a) Calico cat with yellow lustre pincushion, 2¾", Black Mark #1, $28.00-38.00. (b) Calico dog with white shiny-glazed pincushion (could also be used as a toothpick holder), 3¼", Black Mark #38, $28.00-38.00. (c) Tan lustre dog pincushion, 2", Red Mark #1, $28.00-38.00. (d) Same dog pincushion with green and white shiny glaze, 2", Black Mark #1, $28.00-38.00.

Plate 25. (a) White shiny-glazed dog with matte green bucket pincushion, 3¼", Red Mark #18, $18.00-28.00. (b) Shiny-glazed spotted dog with matte-glazed flower pincushion, 2½", Black Mark #19, $18.00-28.00. (c) Brown shiny-glazed dog with yellow matte-glazed bucket pincushion, 3¼", Red Mark #1, $18.00-28.00.

Plate 26. (a) Spotted dog pincushion (with different colored spots from Plate 25b), 2½", Black Mark #1, $18.00-28.00. (b) Spotted frowning dog pincushion, 2¼", Red Mark #1, $18.00-28.00. (c) Tan lustre frowning dog pincushion, 2¼", Red Mark #1, $18.00-28.00.

Plate 27. Yellow, orange and white shiny-glazed card suit dog pincushions. (a) Club, 3", Black Mark #1, $20.00-30.00. (b) Diamond, 2¾", Black Mark #1, $20.00-30.00.

Plate 28. (a) White shiny-glazed animal with green eyes and tan lustre pincushion, 3¼", Black Mark #1, $20.00-30.00. (b) Girl dog with yellow dress and eyes to match and tan lustre pincushion, 3¼", Black Mark #1, $20.00-30.00.

Plate 29. (a) Small calico dog with lolling tongue pincushion, 2¾", Black Mark #1, $28.00-38.00. (b) White shiny-glazed sad dog toothbrush holder, 4¾", Black Mark #1, $85.00-125.00. (c) Big calico dog with lolling tongue toothbrush holder, 4¾", Black Mark #1, $85.00-125.00.

Place 30. (a) Tan lustre bird with yellow lustre heart card suit pincushion, 3", Black Mark #1, $18.00-28.00. (b) Green, orange and beige shiny-glazed foo dog pincushion, 3", Blind Mark #1, $18.00-28.00.

Plate 31. (a) Orange shiny-glazed dog pincushion, 2½", Blind Mark #1, $18.00-28.00. (b) Yellow lustre dog pincushion, 2½", Black Mark #1 and Blind Mark #1, $18.00-28.00. (c) Tan lustre dog pincushion, 2½", Black Mark #1, $18.00-28.00. (d) Gray shiny-glazed dog pincushion, 1¾", Blind Mark #1, $18.00-28.00.

Plate 32. (a) Long-legged man pincushion in multicolored shiny glaze and tan lustre, 2¾", Red Mark #1 and Blind Mark #1, $30.00-40.00. (b) Man with bird on head pincushion in multicolored shiny glaze and blue lustre, 5", Blue Mark #1 and Blind Mark #1, $30.00-40.00. (c) Seated boy pincushion in multicolored lustre, 2¾", Red Mark #1 and Blind Mark #1, $30.00-40.00.

Plate 33. Cat pincushions in orange and green matte glazes, both 3", both Red Mark #1, $20.00-30.00 each.

Plate 34. (a) Rabbit with house pincushion in multicolored shiny glazes, 3", no Mark, $18.00-28.00. (b) Airbrushed orange shiny-glazed rabbit looking backwards over yellow lustre pincushion, toothpick or cache pot, 3½", Black Mark #1, $18.00-28.00. (c) White lustre rabbit with green ears pincushion, 2½", Black Mark #1, $18.00-28.00.

Plate 35. Art Deco airbrushed animal pincushions. (a) Red horse, 2¾", Red Mark #1, $18.00-28.00. (b) Blue elephant, 2¼" Red Mark #1, $18.00-28.00. (c) Green camel, 2½", Red Mark #1, $18.00-28.00.

Plate 36. (a) Orange and black shiny-glazed scottie dog with top hat pincushion, 3½", Handwritten "June 23, 1940, Earling & Melba, Jantzen" (Jantzen Beach was an amusement park in Portland, Oregon), Black Mark #38, $25.00-35.00. (b) Shiny-glazed animal on tan lustre shoe pincushion, 3¾", Black Mark #1, $18.00-28.00.

Plate 37. (a) Calico horse with tan lustre pincushion, 3½", Black Mark #1, $28.00-38.00. (b) White lustre camel with basket pincushion, 3¼", Red Mark #1, $18.00-28.00.

Plate 38. (a) Tan lustre cow pincushion, 2¼", Black Mark #1, $18.00-28.00. (b) Tan lustre duck pincushion, 2", Black Mark #2, $18.00-28.00.

The Volstead Act outlawed liquor in America in 1919. When alcohol became legal again in 1933, there was a big influx of accessories to dress up drinking. The most popular and plentiful cocktail sets were of American-made glassware.

The Japanese ceramics manufacturers never quite caught up with the American glass products, but they did contribute ceramic liquor flasks, decanters—usually figural and sometimes accompanied by a set of shot glasses—and a few Tom and Jerry sets.

And what went better with drinking than smoking? The Japanese beat the Americans all hollow in the production of smoking paraphernalia. Ceramic ashtrays were produced both as singles and in sets of four. Smoking sets, including ashtrays, match holders and cigarette holders on matching ceramic trays, were also very much in demand.

As in so many other areas, the Japanese were imitators as well as innovators in the creation of smoking and drinking items. Many collectors like to find examples of both the German or Czechoslovakian originals and the Japanese "knock-offs."

In America's current moral climate, smoking and drinking are neither healthy nor politically correct. As smoking and drinking accessories are produced in ever-decreasing numbers, values of older items can only increase!

Liquor Flasks

Plate 39. (a) Rare Bisque flask inscribed "Life Preserver," 4¾", Black Mark #38, $95.00-150.00. (b) Green and tan lustre flask inscribed "Just a Little Nip, Souvenir of Hollywood, Calif.," 4", Red Mark #65, $40.00-60.00.

Plate 40. (a) Tan and orange lustre flask inscribed "His Masters Breoth, (sic)," 3¾", Black Mark #1, $75.00-125.00. (b) Tan lustre flask inscribed "A Little Scotch," 4", Black Mark #1, $55.00-85.00. (c) Tan and orange lustre flask inscribed "A Wee Scotch, Old Whisky (sic)," 4", Black Mark #1 and Blind Mark #38, $75.00-125.00.

Plate 41. Matte glazed cowboy decanter 7¼", with six yellow and opal lustre shot glasses, all Black Mark #1, $75.00-100.00 set.

Plate 42. German "prototype" flask with six shot glasses. There's probably a similar Japanese one out there somewhere. $85.00-$105.00 set.

Plate 43. Bisque dog with brown-glazed flask inscribed "All's Well That Ends Well," 4¼", Black Mark #1 with "Patent applied for, no. 9634-7," $75.00-125.00.

Plate 44. Shiny-glazed bottle stoppers on a fence, 4¼", all with Red Mark #2, $35.00-50.00. (At first I thought this might be a "marriage" of items, but they actually were made to go together. I have since seen a few more sets.)

Plate 45. Two flasks that originally may have been from condiment sets, but their owners had them in their bars. (a) Yellow lustre cat, 6½", Red Mark #25 $12.00-15.00. (b) Green and yellow lustre duck, 6¼", Red Mark #25, $12.00-15.00.

Ashtrays

If a piece has a cigarette rest or a match striker, it was intended to be an ashtray, even if it looks like something else such as a teabag holder.

Plate 46. Ivory, tan, blue, and green lustre card suit clowns on "canoe" ashtrays, 1½", (a & b) Red Mark #1, (c & d) Red Mark #32, $18.00-28.00 each.

Plate 47. Tan, yellow, lavender, and blue lustre card suit ashtray set— yes! it's really a set even though the pieces are not very similar! At least one of these, the lady with the leopard, was made with the Occupied Japan Mark, so probably the rest of the set also was made with this Mark. All 3", (a) Black Mark #2, (b & c) Black Mark #1, (d) Black Mark #38, $18.00-28.00 each.

Plate 48. Tan and yellow lustre and multicolored shiny-glazed card suit ashtrays showing a smaller size. (a & e are from Plate 47 for illlustration purposes.) (b) Black Mark #1, (c) Black Mark #38, (d) Red Mark #2, $18.00-28.00 each.

Plate 49. Tan lustre card suit stacking ashtrays, all 2½" diameter, all Red Mark #1, $8.00-10.00 each, $30.00-40.00 for a set of 4 with match holder one on top.

Plate 50. Blue and tan lustre card suit elves ashtrays, all 2½". This set also was made with the Occupied Japan Mark. (a & d) Blue Mark #43a, (b & c) Black Mark #1, $12.00-18.00 each.

Plate 51. Green, tan, yellow, and blue card suit hunters ashtrays, all 1½", all Red Mark #1, $18.00-28.00 each.

Plate 52. Tan and blue lustre boxed card suit ashtray set (very similar to a Noritake set), all 1¾" diameter, all Black Mark #52, (box marked Made in Japan), $45.00-70.00 set.

Plate 53. White shiny-glazed boxed card suit ashtray set, all 3¼" long, all Black Mark #1 and Blind Mark #38, $30.00-40.00 set.

Plate 54. Yellow, blue, green, and tan lustre card suit ashtray set, all 3½" wide, all Black Mark #1, $14.00-18.00 each.

Plate 55. Black and orange shiny-glazed card suit animal ashtrays, 1¾", no Mark, $18.00-28.00 each.

Plate 56. Blue, lavender, and tan lustre card suit clown ashtrays, 3¾" long, Red Mark #1 and Blind Mark #1, $18.00-38.00 each.

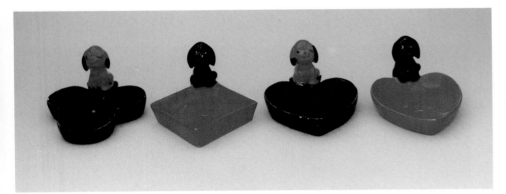

Plate 57. Tan and blue lustre card suit musical mice ashtrays, 1½", Blind Mark #2, $18.00-28.00 each.

Plate 58. "No Trumps" card suit clowns (hands are movable and point to the different card suits). (a) Tan lustre cigarette or card holder, 3¾", Black Mark #1, $35.00-55.00 (b & c) Yellow and blue lustre ashtrays, 2½", both Black Mark #1, $20.00-40.00 each.

Plate 59. (a) Yellow and green lustre card suit clown ashtray with snuffers, 2¾", Red Mark #1 and Blind Mark #1 with incised "A66A," $35.00-70.00. (b) Blue and yellow lustre card suit clown ashtray with snuffers, 2½", Red Mark #1 and Blind Mark #1, $35.00-70.00. (c) Green and yellow lustre card suit clown ashtray, 2¾", Red Mark #1, $35.00-70.00.

Plate 60. (a) Tan lustre with blue shiny-glazed card suit clown ashtray, 2½", Black Mark #2, $35.00-70.00. (b) Cinnamon and blue shiny-glazed card suit clown ashtray, 2½", Red Mark #1, $35.00-70.00.

Plate 61. (a) Blue lustre card suit clown ashtray, 1¾", Black Mark #1, $20.00-36.00. (b) Tan and blue lustre card suit girl ashtray, 1½", Black Mark #1, $20.00-36.00. Blue lustre card suit girl ashtray, 1¾", Black Mark #1, $20.00-36.00.

Plate 62. Blue and tan lustre card suit clown ashtrays pictured in a pre-World War II Butler Brothers Catalog for $9.60/gross wholesale, 10¢ each retail. (a) 2¾", Black Mark #1, $20.00-36.00. (b) 2½", Black Mark #1, $20.00-36.00.

Plate 63. Blue and tan lustre card suit ashtrays. (a) 3¼", Red Mark #1, $12.00-19.00. (b) 2¾", Red Mark #52, $12.00-19.00.

Plate 64. White shiny-glazed card suit cat ashtrays. (a) 3¾", (b) 3½", both Blind Mark #1 with incised "199," $15.00-25.00 each.

Plate 65. White shiny-glazed card suit musical animal with dice and hearts cigarette holders or cache pots, both 2", all Black Mark #1, $19.00-30.00 each.

Plate 66. Yellow, red, and green shiny-glazed card suit musical animals with dice ashtrays, both 3¼", both Red Mark #1, $20.00-30.00 each.

Plate 67. Card suit birdhouse ashtrays. (a) Tan lustre and orange shiny-glazed, inscribed "Roseburg, Oregon." (b) Tan and white lustre. Both 2", both Red Mark #1 and Blind Mark #1, $15.00-22.00 each.

Plate 68. (a) Tan lustre and brown shiny-glazed card suit wolf ashtray, 2¼", Red Mark #1, $12.00-22.00. (b) Yellow lustre card suit mystery animal ashtray, 2", Black Mark #38, $12.00-22.00.

Plate 69. (a) White shiny-glazed card suit clown ashtray, 1¾", Black Mark #1, $20.00-36.00. (b) Blue lustre and white shiny-glazed card suit donkey ashtray (this one and #70. (a) were in the Fall 1933 Sears catalog as part of a four-piece set for 15¢ per set), 1½", Red Mark #1 and Blind Mark #1, $15.00-25.00.

Plate 70. (a) Yellow lustre and white shiny-glazed card suit dog ashtray, 1½", Red Mark #1, $15.00-25.00. (b) Tan lustre and white shiny-glazed card suit mystery animal ashtray, 1½", Black Mark #1, $15.00-25.00.

Plate 71. (a) Orange and blue lustre card suit calico dog ashtray, 2¾", Black Mark #1, $18.00-28.00. (b) White lustre and green matte-glazed card suit saxophonist ashtray, 1½", Blind Mark #1, $15.00-25.00.

Plate 72. (a) Tan lustre card suit standing clown ashtray, 2½", Black Mark #2, $20.00-36.00. (b) Orange and green lustre reclining card suit clown ashtray, 2½", Red Mark #1; as shown, $18.00-36.00; with set of three additional stacking ashtrays, $40.00-95.00.

Plate 73. (a) Yellow and orange lustre card suit dog ashtray. (b) Yellow and tan lustre card suit man ashtray. (c) Blue and green lustre woman ashtray. All 3¾" long, all Red Mark #1 and Blind Mark #1, $12.00-25.00 each.

Plate 74. (a) Tan lustre card suit man ashtray (same figure as Plate #73.b), 1½", Red Mark #40, $11.00-23.00 (b) Blue and green lustre card suit clown ashtray, 3" diameter, Black Mark #40, "FOREIGN," which means it was exported to a country other than America, $11.00-23.00.

Plate 75. (a) Tan and blue lustre card suit bird ashtray (very similar to Noritake pieces, but not identical), 4" wide, Black Mark #1, $12.00-23.00. (b) Brown and white shiny-glazed card suit dog family ashtray, 2", Blind Mark #1, $12.00-23.00. (c) Green lustre ashtray with silhouette panels, 3" wide, Red Mark #1, $9.00-19.00.

Plate 76. Card suit animal ashtrays. (a) Yellow lustre musical pig. (b) Tan lustre musical pig. Both 2½", both Red Mark #1, $18.00-28.00 each. (c) Multicolored elephant, 3", Black Mark #1, $15.00-23.00 each.

Plate 77. (a) Yellow lustre card suit ashtray, 4" long, Black Mark #1, $12.00-22.00. (b) Shiny-glazed face with green bowtie ashtray, 3" long, no Mark, $12.00-22.00.

Plate 78. (a) Tan lustre card suit with musical dog ashtray, 2¾", Black Mark #38, $15.00-23.00. (b) Shiny-glazed dog cigarette holder or cache pot, 3½", Black Mark #2, $18.00-28.00.

Plate 79. Card suit musical animal ashtrays. (a) Yellow lustre mouse. (b) Tan lustre cat. Both 3½", both Red Mark #1, $15.00-25.00 each.

Plate 80. (a) Green and orange lustre Noritake ashtray, 3" diameter, Red Mark #53, $28.00-38.00. (b) White shiny-glazed hand ashtray, 3" wide, Blind Mark #2, $12.00-22.00. (c) Tan and green lustre card suit ashtray, 3" long, Red Mark #1, $12.00-18.00.

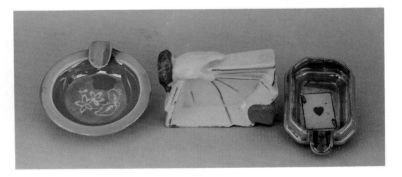

Plate 81. (a) Blue lustre card suit dog ashtray, 4¼", Red Mark #18 and Blind Mark #18, $15.00-25.00. (b) Green-glazed frog with white lustre belly ashtray, 3", Red Mark #1, $12.00-22.00.

Plate 89. (a) Calico dog with tan lustre ashtray with snuffer and matchbox holder, 3", Black Mark #1, $20.00-30.00. (b) Orange ashtray with white cat and blue and yellow cigarette holder, 2¼", Red Mark #1, $30.00-50.00. (c) Orange ashtray with white scottie, 3¼", Black Mark #1, $15.00-25.00.

Plate 90. (a) Blue lustre ashtray with green frog chasing yellow duck, 3", no Mark but with handwritten "1926" on the bottom, $18.00-28.00. (b) Green with white lustre ashtray with dog, 2½", Red Mark #1, $18.00-28.00.

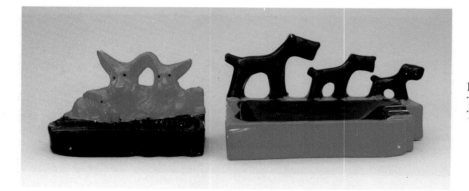

Plate 91. Orange- and black-glazed dog ashtrays. (a) Two scotties, 2¾", Black Mark #1, $18.00-28.00. (b) Three Art Deco dogs, 3", Red Mark #1, $18.00-28.00.

Plate 92. (a) Orange ashtray with brown and white dog. (b) Orange ashtray with black and white dog. Both 2¾", both Red Mark #1, $18.00-28.00 each.

Plate 93. (a) Green with white lustre dog ashtray, 2¼", Red Mark #2, $15.00-25.00. (b) Green with calico dachshund ashtray, 3", Black Mark #1, $18.00-28.00. (c) Yellow and tan lustre dog ashtray, 2¼", Black Mark #1, $18.00-28.00.

Plate 94. (a) Tan lustre with pelican ashtray and snuffers, 2¾", Red Mark #1, $15.00-25.00 (b) Yellow and white lustre dog ashtray with snuffers, 2¼", Black Mark #2, $15.00-25.00 (c) Blue and tan lustre dog ashtray with snuffers, 2½", Black Mark #1, $15.00-25.00.

Plate 95. (a) Orange and tan lustre ashtray with spotted dog and snuffers, 3½", Black Mark #1, $15.00-25.00. (b) Tan lustre ashtray with spotted dog and snuffers, 2½", Black Mark #1, $15.00-25.00.

Plate 96. (a) Tan lustre ashtray with snuffers and yellow ducks, 2", Red Mark #1 and Blind Mark #1, $15.00-25.00. (b) Yellow lustre ashtray with snuffers and dog, 2", Red Mark #2, $15.00-25.00. (c) Yellow and tan lustre ashtray with dog and snuffers, 2½", Black Mark #1, $15.00-25.00. (d) Tan lustre ashtray with calico dog and snuffers, 2½", Red Mark #1, $18.00-28.00.

Plate 97. (a) Blue lustre ashtray with dog and

Plate 113. (a) Tan lustre ashtray with "disk" dog, 3¼", Red Mark #1, $25.00-35.00. (b) Yellow and green lustre pelican ashtray with snuffer holes on back, 3¼", Red Mark #1, $25.00-35.00.

Plate 114. (a) Yellow lustre duck family ashtray with snuffers, 2½", Red Mark #1 and Blind Mark #1, $15.00-25.00. (b) Tan and yellow lustre swan ashtray with snuffers, 2¼", Red Mark #1, $15.00-25.00.

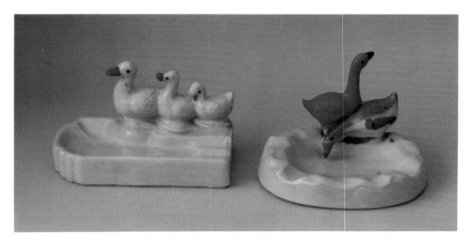

Plate 115. (a) Yellow and white lustre duck trio ashtray, 2½", Black Mark #1, $15.00-25.00. (b) Tan lustre ashtray with red and blue geese, 2¾", Black Mark #1, $15.00-25.00.

Plate 116. (a) Tan and white lustre ashtray with dog and clock, 1¾", Black Mark #1, $15.00-25.00. (b) Orange and blue lustre ashtray with cat and clock, 2", Red Mark #1, $15.00-25.00.

Plate 117. (a) Tan lustre ashtray with dog and life preserver, 2½", Red Mark #1, $15.00-25.00. (b) White shiny-glazed ashtray with squirrel and tree snuffers, 2¼", Black Mark #2, $15.00-25.00. (c) Tan lustre ashtray with fishbowl ornament and snuffers, 2¾", Red Mark #1, $15.00-25.00.

Plate 118. (a) Green shiny-glazed camel ashtray, 3¼", Black Mark #1, $15.00-25.00. (b & c) Green and maroon rhino ashtrays, both 2½", both Black Mark #1, $15.00-25.00 each.

Plate 119. (a) White and tan lustre cowboy ashtray with snuffer belt, 5¼", Black Mark #1, $40.00-55.00. (b) Calico clown on white-glazed ashtray with snuffers, 3½", Black Mark #1 and Blind Mark #1, $30.00-55.00.

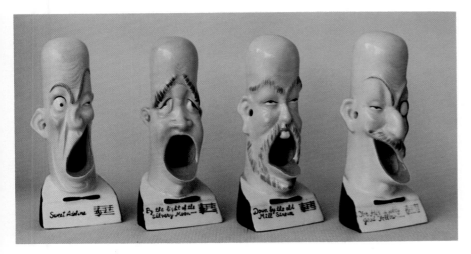

Plate 120. Barbershop quartet "smoker" ashtrays inscribed "Sweet Adeline," "By the light of the Silvery Moon," "Down by the old Mill Stream," and "For He's a jolly good Fellow," 5", Label #60, $65.00-125.00 each. (There are German versions of these ashtrays. The glaze is slightly different, and they are incised with numbers on the underside. If there are no numbers and no labels, then the piece is Japanese and the labels have been removed. The German ashtrays are now priced about the same as the Japanese ones.)

Plate 121. Yellow and green shiny-glazed donkey ashtray with snuffers, 5", Black Mark #1, $18.00-28.00.

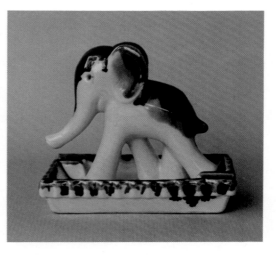

Plate 122. Yellow and green shiny-glazed elephant ashtray, 3¾", Black Mark #1, $18.00-28.00.

Plate 123. (a) Blue lustre caped flapper ashtray, 4¾" long, Black Mark #1 and Blind Mark #1, $35.00-65.00. (b) Yellow lustre caped flapper (similar to #1 but the feet and legs are different), 4¼", Blind Mark #1, $35.00-65.00. (c) Tan lustre clown, 4½", Red Mark #1, $35.00-65.00.

Plate 124. (a) Blue lustre ashtray with saxophonist and snuffers, inscribed "Souvenir of Tampa, Florida," Black Mark #1, $60.00-75.00. (b) White shiny-glazed ashtray with dice player and snuffers, 4¼", Black Mark #1 and Blind Mark #1, $75.00-95.00.

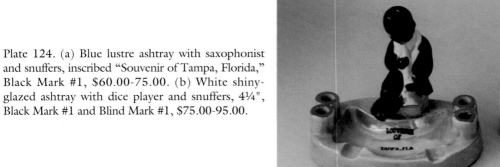

Plate 125. (a) White lustre ashtray with horn player, 2", Black Mark #1, $30.00-40.00. (b) Tan lustre commode ashtray inscribed "Next," 1½", Black Mark #1, $25.00-35.00.

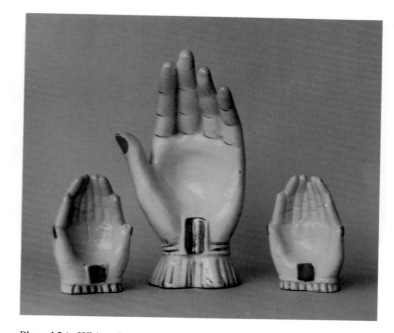

Plate 126. White shiny-glazed hand ashtrays. (a & c) pairs of small cupped hands, 2¾, Blind Mark #2, $15.00-20.00 each. (b) Large single hand, 5½", Red Mark #2, $18.00-25.00.

Plate 127. Pig trio ashtrays, all 2¾", all Black Mark #38, $18.00-25.00 each.

Plate 128. Bird ashtray set with striker bottoms, all Red Mark #2 and Blind Mark #1. (a) White lustre peacock 3¼". (b) Tan lustre owl 3¼". (c) Yellow lustre pelican 3". (d) Blue lustre swan 3". $18.00-25.00 each.

Plate 136. (a) Green lustre ashtray with card panels (shown in the Spring 1933 Sears catalog for 10¢), 2½", Blind Mark #38, $16.00-26.00. (b) Green and white lustre hand and dice ashtray on book, 3½", Black Mark #1, $25.00-35.00. (c) Orange lustre ashtray, 2½", Red Mark #11, $15.00-20.00.

Plate 137. Black shiny-glazed "smoker" locomotive ashtray, 3¼", Blind Mark #1, $15.00-25.00.

Plate 138. (a) Tan lustre ashtray, 1¼", Red Mark #1, $12.00-18.00. (b) Blue and tan lustre ashtray with cigarette rest, 1½", Black Mark #32, $12.00-18.00.

Plate 139. Three unmarked pieces. (a) White shiny-glazed ashtray with mandolin player (looks too "fine" to be Japanese—may be German), 3½", $18.00-28.00 if Japanese, $25.00-35.00 if German. (b) Yellow lustre penguin stamp moistener, 3¼", $30.00-45.00. (c) Blue and white lustre ashtray with lion, inscribed "HIGH 1383, TYEE WOOD & COAL LTD," $18.00-28.00.

Smoking Paraphernalia

If people really wanted to get fancy about smoking—and often they did—lots of accessories were available. Cigarette jars, animals with cigarette carriers, and cigarette vases (vessels that were intended for cigarettes but could also be used for playing cards or flowers) were all popular choices.

Plate 140. Cream and green lustre smoking set on matching tray. Tray 11" long, cigarette jar 5", match holder with ashtray, 3¼". All Black Mark #56, $70.00-95.00 set.

Plate 141. Orange lustre Noritake smoking set on matching tray with Art Deco lady with greyhound and street scene. Tray 7" long, no Mark. Match holder 2", Red Mark #2. Cigarette holder 2¼", Red Mark #53. $250.00-325.00 set.

Plate 142. Blue lustre Noritake smoking set with butterflies on matching tray. Tray 7¼", Red Mark #53. Cigarette vase 3", Red Mark #53. Match holder 2¼", Red Mark #2. (There is a matching ashtray that completes this set.) $35.00-55.00 per piece.

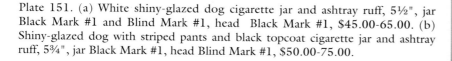

Plate 150. (a) Calico clown dog cigarette jar and ashtray ruff, 6¼", Black Mark #1, $50.00-75.00. (b) White shiny-glazed spotted dog cigarette jar, 5", Black Mark #1, $45.00-65.00.

Plate 151. (a) White shiny-glazed dog cigarette jar and ashtray ruff, 5½", jar Black Mark #1 and Blind Mark #1, head Black Mark #1, $45.00-65.00. (b) Shiny-glazed dog with striped pants and black topcoat cigarette jar and ashtray ruff, 5¾", jar Black Mark #1, head Blind Mark #1, $50.00-75.00.

Plate 152. Rare clown cigarette, humidor or candy jar in green lustre with orange and yellow trim, 5½", Black Mark #1, $95.00-165.00.

Plate 153. Owl cigarette jar or small humidor in yellow matte glaze, 5", Red Mark #20, $60.00-85.00.

Plate 154. (a) Green and orange crackle-glazed humidor, 5", Red Mark #25, $40.00-55.00. (b) Cream and green crackle-glazed humidor, 5½", Red Mark #25, $45.00-65.00.

Plate 155. Green and yellow crackle-glazed humidor, 6", Red Mark #25, $45.00-65.00.

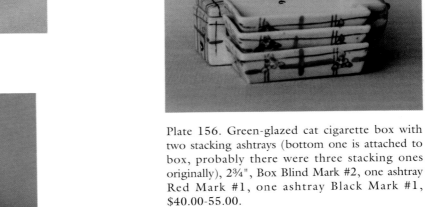

Plate 156. Green-glazed cat cigarette box with two stacking ashtrays (bottom one is attached to box, probably there were three stacking ones originally), 2¾", Box Blind Mark #2, one ashtray Red Mark #1, one ashtray Black Mark #1, $40.00-55.00.

Plate 157. Green and orange-glazed cigarette box with attached ashtray, match holder, and elephant knob, 4½", Black Mark #1, $45.00-60.00.

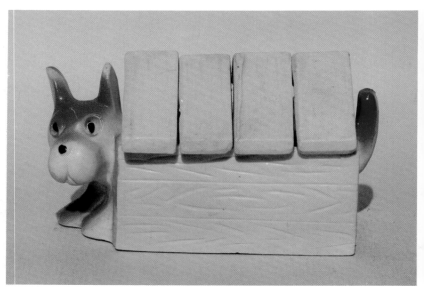

Plate 158. Tan lustre dog cigarette holder with two stacking ashtrays (there were probably four originally), 2¾", all pieces Red Mark #1, $20.00-30.00 as found ($35.00-50.00 with all four ashtrays).

Plate 159. Dog house cigarette box with four-ashtray roof in yellow and brown matte glazes, 3", all pieces Black Mark #1, $35.00-55.00.

Plate 160. Brown and white-glazed scottie dog cigarette box with four stacking ashtrays, 4¼", all pieces Black Mark #1, $50.00-60.00.

Plate 161. Art Deco green, yellow and cream-glazed cigarette box with mystery animal knob, 5", Red Mark #1 with number "CB10SS," $55.00-80.00.

Incense Burners and Match Holders

The really thoughtful pre-World War II hostess provided an incense burner to freshen the air after smoking, and incense burners became popular accessories even in non-smoking households.

Considering the astronomical number of ashtrays the Japanese produced, one might expect a large number of matchholders. This is not the case. A number of them were included in smoking sets. The figural ones are collected as a separate category, so perhaps that's why they are so scarce.

Plate 162. (a) Blue and tan lustre incense burner with cavity in back for burning incense, hole in mouth for smoke to come out, joss stick holes on toes, and attached tray, 3¼", Red Mark #52, $40.00-65.00. (b) Bisque incense burner with cavity in back for burning incense and joss stick holes on head and toes, 3.5", Red Mark #2, $30.00-50.00.

Plate 163. (a) Blue and white lustre Indian chief match or cigarette holder with tray but no striker grooves, 4", Red Mark #52, $40.00-65.00. (b) Blue, yellow, and white lustre elephant and monkey rider incense burner (monkey comes off and burning chamber is on elephant's back), 5", Black Mark #1, $40.00-65.00.

Plate 164. Tan, yellow, and white lustre pair of match holders with match striker grooves, buckets, and attached trays. 3¼", Black Mark #1, $25.00-35.00 each.

Plate 165. Three red, black, yellow, and blue shiny-glazed incense burners with cavities in back for burning incense and pots with smoke holes in front. There are quite a few other sizes and versions of these three figures. There are also versions of the Oriental with the Occupied Japan mark. (a) Mexican, 3¾", Red Mark #2, $28.00-36.00. (b) Indian 5¾", Black Mark #41, $28.00-36.00. (c) Oriental, 3¾", Red Mark #1, $18.00-28.00.

Plate 201. (a) Boy with trunk toothbrush holder in blue, green and white lustre, 4¼", red MADE IN GERMANY, (Although not an exact duplicate, this certainly could have been the inspiration for the boys in plates 198 and 199), $95.00-135.00. (b) Bisque Humpty Dumpty toothbrush holder, 5¼", Blind Stamped "Patent Pending" with no other marking, $95.00-135.00.

Plate 202. (a) Elephant toothbrush holder in blue, yellow, and brown shiny glazes, 3¾", Blind Mark #1 with unclear incised words that may read "Yankly or Yanklo Made," $85.00-125.00. (b) Soccer player toothbrush holder and tube tray in white, green, red, and black shiny glazes, 4¾", no Mark, $85.00-125.00.

Plate 203. Two 6½" rabbit toothbrush holders with tube trays (a) red, yellow and green shiny glazes with rhinestone buttons, Red Mark #44, $85.00-125.00. (b) Same glazes but no rhinestones, Red Mark #48, $85.00-125.00.

Plate 204. Two animal toothbrush holders. (a) Cat in yellow shiny glaze, 5¾", Red Mark #43, $85.00-125.00. (b) Donkey in orange shiny glaze, 6½", Red Mark #43, $85.00-125.00.

Plate 205. (a) Duck toothbrush holder in yellow shiny glaze, 5¼", Black Mark #63, $85.00-125.00. (b) Duck toothbrush holder with tube tray in orange shiny glaze, 5¾", Black Mark #1 and Blind Mark #1, $85.00-125.00.

Plate 206. (a) Rare scottie dog card game toothbrush holder with tube tray in orange, white, and black shiny glazes, 4½", Red Mark #44, $85.00-125.00. (b) Scottie dog toothbrush holder with tube tray in gray and green shiny glazes, 6½" Red Mark #43, $85.00-125.00.

Plate 207. (a) Elephant toothbrush holder with tube tray in black and pink shiny glazes, 5", Black Mark #1, $85.00-125.00. (b) Giraffe toothbrush holder with tube tray in tan and white shiny glazes, 6", Black Mark #2, $85.00-125.00.

Plate 208. (a) Elephant toothbrush holder with tube tray in blue, yellow, and orange lustre glazes, 5½", Red Mark #1, $85.00-125.00. (b) Frog with banjo toothbrush holder with tube tray in gray and green matte glazes, 6", Red Mark #44, $85.00-125.00.

Plate 209. Pair of doggie toothbrush holders with tube trays showing color variations in blue shiny glazes from the same factory. Both 6", both Red Mark #43, $85.00-125.00 each.

Plate 210. (a) Bull toothbrush holder in blue and tan lustre, 4¼", Black Mark #43, $85.00-125.00. (b) Baby bull toothbrush holder in white lustre, 3½", Red Mark #1, $85.00-125.00. (c) Cat toothbrush holder in tan and white lustre, 4¼", Red Mark #43, $85.00-125.00.

Plate 211. Calico dog toothbrush holders. (a) 4", Red Mark #43, $90.00-130.00. (b) 5", Black Mark #1, $90.00-130.00.

Plate 212. Calico cat toothbrush holders with tube trays. (a) 4½", Red Mark #1, $90.00-130.00. (b) 5¾", Black Mark #1, $90.00-130.00.

Plate 213. (a) Pig toothbrush holder in orange shiny glaze, 3", Red Mark #65, $85.00-125.00. (b) Lion toothbrush holder in orange and white lustre, 3½", Black Mark #1, $85.00-125.00.

Plate 214. (a) Bear toothbrush holder in brown shiny glaze inscribed "BEAR IN MIND," 7", no Mark (has felt glued to bottom hiding Mark, if any), $85.00-125.00. (b) Bear toothbrush holder with tube tray in brown and green shiny glazes, 5¾", Red Mark #44, $85.00-125.00.

Plate 215. (a) Bird toothbrush holder in red, black, and white shiny glazes, 3¼", Red Mark #1, $85.00-125.00. (b) Penguin toothbrush holder with tube tray in blue, white, and black shiny glazes, 5½", Black Mark #2, $85.00-125.00.

Plate 228. (a) Comical bathing suit couple on ashtray in white lustre inscribed "She's As Nice A Gal as Y'd Want T'Meet, But She Loves To Ride In The Rumble Seat," 3½", Black Mark #1, $35.00-50.00. (b) Bathing beauty in orange lustre suit on mottled green shiny-glazed ashtray, 3", Red Mark #1, $35.00-50.00.

Plate 229. (a) Bathing beauty in orange suit on white lustre shell ashtray, 3¾", Red Mark #1, $45.00-65.00. (b) Bathing beauty in maroon suit on white lustre shell vase, 3¾", Red Mark #1, $45.00-65.00.

Plate 230. (a) Bathing beauty in orange suit on white lustre shell ashtray, 3", Red Mark #1, $45.00-65.00. (b) Bathing beauty in green suit on white lustre shell vase, 3¼", Red Mark #1, $45.00-65.00.

Plate 231. (a) Comical bathing beauty in orange suit with white lustre scale on blue lustre ashtray inscribed "OH THE SCALE MUST BE WRONG," 3½", Mark scratched off, $30.00-40.00. (b) Ladies with red and green shiny-glazed drawers and blowing skirts on tan lustre pin tray, 3¾", Black Mark #1, $25.00-35.00.

Plate 232. (a) Lustre pin tray with bathing beauty in cobalt suit, 1¾", no Mark, $20.00-30.00. (b) Bathing beauty in green suit on white lustre ashtray, 1½", Black Mark #1, $25.00-35.00.

Plate 233. Rare, large bisque nude lady on starfish, 4½", Black Mark #1, $75.00-125.00.

Plate 234. Comical bisque bathing suit couples. (a) Inscribed "LOVER COME BACK TO ME," 4½", Black Mark #1, $35.00-50.00. (b) Inscribed "I NEVER FELT SUCH AN ASS IN MY LIFE," 3½", Red Mark #1, $35.00-50.00.

Plate 235. Two ladies that look as though they've spent considerable time in fishbowls. (a) Mermaid on seahorse in white, green, and orange shiny glazes, 3¼", Red Mark #2, $5.00 as found ($20.00-30.00 if glazes were intact.). (b) Bathing beauty in green suit on tan lustre turtle, 2½", Red Mark #1 and Blind Mark #1, $5.00 as found. ($20.00-30.00 if glazes were intact.)

Plate 281. Scenic ceramic vase glazed to look like metal, 7½", Gold Mark #1, $25.00-35.00.

Plate 282. Orange shiny-glazed vase with Art Deco motif, 6", Blue Mark #52, $46.00-52.00.

Plate 283. Rare black matte-glazed vase with tan lustre accents and multicolored poppies, 6", Green Mark #21A, $50.00-60.00.

Plate 284. Brown shiny-glazed vase with enameled flowers, 7½", Yellow Mark #1, $18.00-28.00.

Plate 285. Cream crackle-glazed vase with multicolored poppies, 5½", Black Mark #62, $42.00-52.00.

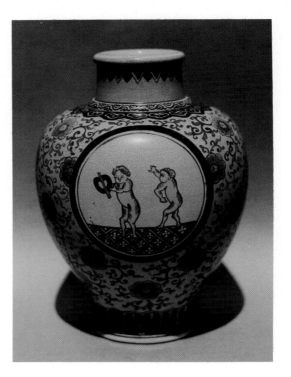

Plate 286. Rare pink vase with yellow panel and multicolored designs, 8¾", (a pre-WWII piece from the Akiyama store), Red Mark #49, $198.00-252.00.

Plate 287. (a) Tan and blue lustre vase, 4¾", Red Mark #10, $22.00-28.00. (b) Tan and blue lustre vase, 5", Red Mark #52, $22.00-28.00.

Plate 288. (a) Tan lustre Noritake vase, 5¼" with gold multicolored motif, Red Mark #53, $75.00-85.00. (b) Tan lustre vase with multicolored scene, 7¼", Red Mark #11, $30.00-50.00.

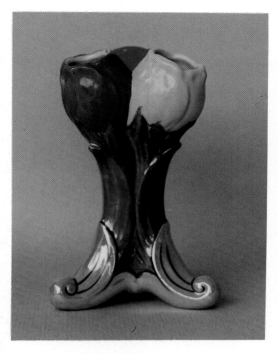

Plate 289. Tan lustre vase with multicolored tulips, 6", Black Mark #1, $30.00-45.00.

Plate 290. Yellow lustre Art Deco vase with red and multicolored motifs, 6½", Black Mark #43, $30.00-48.00.

Plate 291. Flower basket with yellow, blue, and tan lustre glazes, 7", Red Mark #20, $50.00-70.00.

Plate 292. Tan lustre vase with green and multicolored floral panel, 5", Red Mark #20, $27.00-37.00.

Plate 293. Rare multicolored Art Deco vase, 7¼", Blind Mark #1, (a pre-WW II piece from the Akiyama store with original paper label "No. 112, 3.00"), $125.00-138.00.

Plate 294. Rare multicolored Art Deco vase, 5½", Blind Mark #1, (a pre-WW II piece from the Akiyama store), $125.00-138.00.

Plate 295. Rare multicolored Art Deco vase, 5¾", Blind Mark #1, $125.00-138.00.

Plate 296. Very rare and large pair of multicolored Art Deco vases, 9½", Blind Mark #1, (pre-WW II pieces from the Akiyama store with original paper label "No. 121, 6.00"), $150.00-210.00 each.

Plate 327. (a) Cobalt blue mini bud vase with white dog, 4", Black Mark #2, $15.00-20.00. (b) Boxer dog mini bud vase in orange, black and white shiny glazes, 4", Red Mark #11, $15.00-20.00.

Plate 328. (a) Mini bud vase with scottie dogs in white and orange lustre, 4¼", Black Mark #1, $12.00-20.00. (b) Round mini vase in orange lustre, 3", Red Mark #1, $8.00-12.00.

Plate 329. (a) Mini bud vase in yellow lustre with multicolored siesta figure, 3¾", Black Mark #2, $12.00-20.00. (b) Cobalt mini bud vase with white shiny-glazed figure, 3¼", Black Mark #2, $12.00-20.00.

Plate 330. Set of four mini vases, all 2½" except far right 2", all Blind Mark #2, $8.00-12.00 set.

Plate 331. Two "Satsuma-type" mini vases. (a) 3½", Red Mark #41, $12.00-22.00. (b) 2", Red Mark #1, $12.00-22.00.

Plate 332. Pair of "Satsuma-type" mini vases, 2½", (a) Red Mark #43, $12.00-22.00. (b) Red Mark #44, $12.00-22.00.

Plate 333. (a) Flower basket in cream glaze with cobalt and multicolored accents, 4", Black Mark #1, $38.00-48.00. (b) Flower bowl or planter in green glaze, 6" wide, Black Mark #1, $20.00-30.00.

334. Flower bowl in blue and orange lustre with multicolored flowers, 6½" diameter, Red Mark #25, $30.00-52.00.

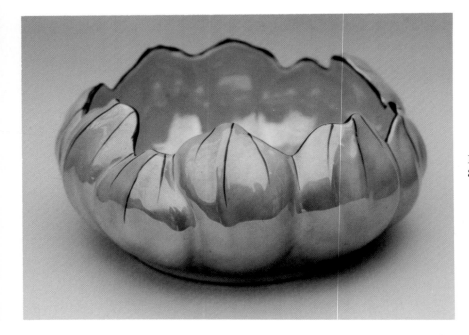

Plate 335. Noritake bowl in blue and orange lustre, 8" diameter, Red Mark #53, $65.00-85.00.

Plate 336. Figural flower hanging vase with attached frog in multicolored lustres. 3¼", Black Mark #1, $40.00-55.00.

Plate 337. (a) Scottie dog wall pocket in orange and black shiny glazes, a major piece due to its subject and large size of 8¾" long. Black Mark #1, $55.00-85.00. (b) Mini scottie dog wall pocket in black and white shiny glazes, 3½", Black Mark #1, $25.00-40.00.

Plate 338. (a) Flowered wall pocket in blue and white lustre with multicolored flowers, 6¼", Black Mark #21a, $40.00-55.00. (b) Narrow wall pocket in cream and orange lustre with multicolored flowers, 6¼", Black Mark #1, $35.00-50.00. (c) Wall pocket with bird in orange lustre with multicolored motif, 6¼" Red Mark #1, $40.00-55.00.

Plate 339. (a) Cuckoo clock wall pocket in multicolored shiny glazes, 5", Black Mark #2, $22.00-32.00. (b) Flowered wall pocket in pink, yellow and green shiny glazes, 6¾", Black Mark #1, $25.00-40.00. (c) Basket wall pocket in orange and black shiny glazes with multicolored flowers, 5½", Blind Mark #1, $25.00-40.00.

Plate 340. (a and c) Dutch boy and girl wall pocket set with cream and tan lustre baskets and multicolored figures, 6½", Black Mark #1 and Blind Mark #1, $60.00-90.00 set. (b) Hawaiian girl wall plaque in orange lustre, 6", Red Mark #25, $40.00-55.00.

Plate 347. Pixies in multicolored shiny glazes. (a) Pixie vase, 4", Red Mark #2, $20.00-28.00. (b) Pixie vase 3¾", Red Mark #2, $20.00-28.00. (c) Pixie wall pocket, 4", Red Mark #9, $20.00-28.00.

Plate 349. Chicken and egg wall pocket, 4¼", Blue Mark #2, $20.00-30.00.

Plate 348. Floral wall pocket with black, red and orange matte glazes (shown with similar decoration in the Spring 1928 Sears Catalog under the brand name Tokanabe for 79¢), 7½", Blind Mark #1, $20.00-30.00.

Plate 350. Colonial lady wall pocket in multiclored shiny glazes (shown in the Fall 1934 Sears catalog for 39¢), 5¾", Green Mark #1, $35.00-50.00.

❧ Cache Pots and Planters ❧

Most Japanese pieces intended for plants are cache pots—without holes for water to drain away. Therefore, many pieces have lime and dirt damage because people rooted plants directly in them instead of using a liner pot. Severe damage affects the value because it is virtually impossible to remove all the stains without marring the glaze. Still, cache pots are about the most reasonably priced items from Japan, so they are usually a bargain in any condition. Planters (with drain holes) also are reasonably priced unless they have an Art Deco motif.

Plate 351. (a) Three Art Deco girls on a cache pot in black and white shiny glaze, 3½", Black Mark #1, $20.00-30.00. (b) Cherub on swan boat cache pot in black and white shiny glazes, 3¼", Black Mark #1, $20.00-30.00.

Plate 352. Rare boy in fez with double cache pots in yellow lustre with multicolored figure, 4", Red Mark #65, $30.00-40.00.

Plate 353. (a) Mandolin player cache pot in green lustre with multicolored figure, 4", Black Mark #1, $15.00-25.00. (b) Man with camel cache pot in tan lustre with multicolored figures, 2½", Black Mark #1, $15.00-25.00.

Plate 389. (a) Man with top hat pincushion in black, orange and blue matte glazes, 4", Blind Mark #1, $30.00-40.00. (b) Man with top hat napkin ring in black and white shiny glazes, 3½", Red Mark #18 and Blind Mark #18, $25.00-35.00. (c) Man with top hat toothpick or pincushion in black and white matte glazes, 3", Black Mark #1, $30.00-40.00.

Plate 390. (a) Man with top hat toothbrush holder in cream lustre with black matte glaze, 4¼", Black Mark #1, $85.00-125.00. (b) Boy with hat and umbrella pincushion in blue lustre with multicolored shiny glazes (shown in the Fall 1932 Sears catalog with a girl pincushion, called "Hans and Gretchen" at 19¢ a pair), 4", Black Mark #1 and Blind Mark #1, $35.00-55.00. (c) Bunny groom figurine in black and white shiny glazes, 3¾", Red Mark #1, $12.00-18.00.

Plate 391. (a) Soldier napkin ring in multicolored shiny glazes, 4¾", Red Mark #2, $25.00-35.00. (b) Marching soldier cache pot in multicolored shiny glazes, 4½", Red Mark #1, $20.00-30.00.

Plate 392. (a) Drumming soldier cache pot in multicolored matte glazes, 4¾", Black Mark #1 and Blind Mark #1, $20.00-30.00. (b) Soldier and lady "hugger" salt and pepper in multicolored matte glazes, 4", $20.00-35.00. (c) Soldier with bugle cache pot in green lustre with multicolored figure, 4", Red Mark #1, $20.00-30.00.

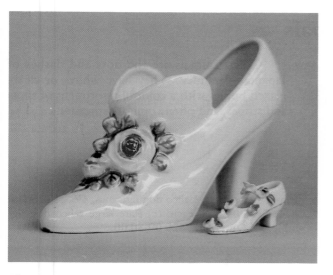

Plate 394. (a) White high heeled shoe in shiny glazes, 1½", Red Mark #2, $18.00-28.00. (b) Boot in tan lustre, 2½", Red Mark #2, $18.00-28.00. (c) Sling back pump in pink and white shiny glazes, 2¾", Red Mark #34, $18.00-28.00.

Plate 393. (a) Big shoe in cream and multicolored shiny glazes, 5", Black Mark #2, $18.00-28.00. (b) Mini shoe in white and multicolored shiny glazes, 1", Green Mark #2, $18.00-28.00.

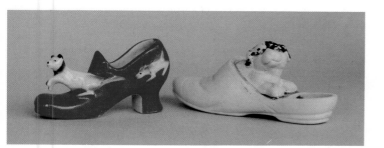

Plate 395. (a) Cat and mouse shoe in orange shiny glaze, 1¾", Red Mark #2, $18.00-28.00. (b) Bisque dog in slipper, 1½", Black Mark #1, $18.00-28.00.

Plate 396. Dog on shoe in black and brown shiny glazes, 2½", Blue Mark #1, $18.00-28.00.

Plate 397. Dog on shoe in black and brown matte glazes, no Mark, 2¼", $18.00-28.00.

Plate 398. (a) Rabbit on shoe in tan lustre, 2¼" long, Made In Occupied Japan, $18.00-28.00. (b) Flowered shoe in tan lustre, 1¾" long, Black Mark #2, $18.00-28.00. (c) Cat and mouse on shoe in tan lustre, 2¼" long, Black Mark #1, $18.00-28.00.

Plate 422. (a) Bonzo-type mustard pot in yellow lustre and black and white shiny glazes, 3¼", Black Mark #1, $40.00-65.00. (b) Bonzo-type ashtray in green matte and white shiny glazes, 1¾", Red Mark #1, $40.00-65.00. (c) Bonzo-type pincushion (opening on back) in black and white shiny glazes, 3¾", Red Mark #1, $45.00-65.00.

Plate 423. Bonzo-type ashtray with cigarette panniers in blue and tan lustre and black and white shiny glazes, 3", Black Mark #1, $50.00-75.00.

Plate 424. Two Bonzo-type toothbrush holders. (a) Black and white shiny glazes with matte orange tummy, Blind Mark #2, inscribed "© The Hinode," 5½", $200.00-300.00. (b) Green and red-glazed with tube tray (shown in the Spring 1932 Sears Catalog under the brand name "Taisho Ware" complete with toothbrush for 29¢), 5½", $200.00-300.00.

Plate 425. Bonzo-type muffineer set in beige and multicolored shiny glazes, 5¼", Black Mark #24, $200.00-275.00 set.

⚶ Orange-Glazed Kitchenware ⚶

Orange matte glaze must have been really popular in the past, because the Japanese seem to have produced more of it than any other single color except white. One reason for this may be that orange is an easy color to fire. Also, America's Fiesta Ware pottery dishes popularized bright colors, including orange (which the Homer Laughlin Company called "red").

A shelf of orange novelties can be a real focal point of a kitchen, and it looks even better with a contrasting color, such as black.

Plate 426. Rare tomato face teapot, 5¾", and cups, 2¾", all Black Mark #50. Set of teapot and four cups, $70.00-85.00.

Plate 427. (a) Tomato face salt and pepper, 2¾", Black Mark #2, $18.00-25.00. (b) Flowered salt and pepper, 2½", Black Mark #2, $12.00-18.00.

Plate 428. (a) Rare tomato butter dish, 3¼", Black Mark #14 and Patent No. 103032, $40.00-55.00. (b) Tomato salt and pepper, 2", Black Mark #14 and Patent No. 69429, $12.00-18.00.

Plate 443. Lefton China lady, 9", Gold Mark #58, $85.00-125.00. (Lefton China is a separate category of Japanese collectibles. They have been in business since 1940.)

Plate 444. Rare skier figurine in multicolored matte glazes, 7¾", Black Mark #1, $50.00-60.00.

Plate 445. Pair of colonials in pink multicolored shiny glazes, 9½", Blue paper label with Mark #2, $60.00-85.00 pair.

Plate 446. Colonial figural piece with mirror in multicolored shiny glazes, 7½", Black Mark #1, $25.00-40.00.

Plate 447. Pair of clown figurines in cinnamon and yellow matte glazes (also made as salt and peppers), 1¾" and 1½", both Black Mark #2, $20.00-30.00 pair.

Plate 448. Pair of clown figurines in multicolored shiny glazes. (a) 4¾", Red Mark #2, $15.00-20.00. (b) 3½", Black Mark #1, $15.00-20.00.

Plate 449. Pair of musicians in yellow and multicolored shiny glazes, 4½", both Red Mark #51, $18.00-28.00 each.

Plate 450. Three dog figural pieces. (a) Blue and tan lustre dogs in bucket, 3¼", Black Mark #1, $15.00-20.00. (b) Dogs and watering can in multicolored matte glazes, 2¼", Red Mark #2, $15.00-20.00. (c) Dogs and pail in multicolored matte glazes, 2½", Red Mark #2, $15.00-20.00.

Plate 465. (a) Skirtholder powder jar in yellow and blue lustre, 5½", Black Mark #1, $75.00-125.00. (b) Clown powder jar in blue, tan, and green lustre, 5¼", Black Mark #1, $75.00-125.00.

Plate 466. Rare clown powder jar in orange and pink lustre with multicolored figure, 7¼", Red Mark #1, $130.00-230.00.

Plate 467. Clown powder jar in cream and multi-colored shiny glazes, 5½", Black Mark #1, $50.00-75.00.

Plate 468. Powder jar in green and orange airbrushed glazes, 2½", Black Mark #1 and Blind Mark #1, $45.00-80.00.

Plate 469. Rare bird soapdish or pin tray in blue and tan lustre with red figure, 4½" wide, Green Mark #20, $25.00-35.00.

Plate 470. (a) Elephant soapdish in green matte glaze, 3", Black Mark #1, $20.00-30.00. (b) Elephant pin tray in lavender and white matte glazes, 2¾", Blue Mark #12, $20.00-30.00. (c) Elephant pin tray in blue and tan lustre, 1¾", Black Mark #1 and Blind Mark #1, $20.00-30.00.

Plate 471. (a) Hair receiver in cobalt and multicolored shiny glazes, 2¼", Green Mark #1, $55.00-65.00. (b) Hair receiver in cream and multicolored matte glazes, 2½", Blue Mark #1, $55.00-65.00.

Plate 472. (a) Hair receiver with violets in multicolored shiny glazes, 2¾", Green Mark #1, $55.00-65.00. (b) Geisha Girl hair receiver in red and multicolored glazes, 2½", Red Mark #1, $60.00-75.00.

Plate 496. Bird bookends in multicolored shiny glazes (a strange configuration—the right bird is backwards), 4", Blind Mark #2, $20.00-35.00 pair.

Plate 497. Dog bookends in green shiny glaze, inscribed (a pre-WWII set from an acquaintance of the owner), 3¾", Black Mark #1, $25.00-40.00 pair.

Plate 498. (a) Cat and book bookends in multicolored shiny glazes, 5", Red Mark #2, $40.00-60.00 pair. (b) Dog bookend in multicolored shiny glazes, 4¾", Red Mark #1 and Blind Mark #1, $15.00-20.00.

Plate 499. Imitation "Hummel" girl and boy bookends in multicolored shiny glazes, 5¾", Red Mark #44, $45.00-75.00 pair.

Plate 500. Ladies and gentlemen bookends in yellow and lavender shiny glazes, 5¼", Red Mark #1, $25.00-45.00 pair.

Plate 501. Lady bookend in tan lustre with matte-glazed multicolored figure, 6", Black Mark #1, $15.00-20.00.

Plate 502. Rare Egyptian girl incense burner, 5¾", Red Mark #65, $65.00-95.00.

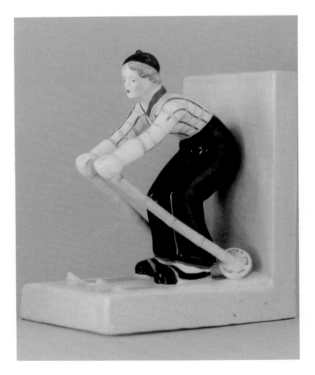

Plate 503. Rare lady skier bookend in multicolored matte glazes, 6", Red Mark #1, $15.00-20.00.

⚐ Holidays ⚐

Holiday ceramic items from Japan were not as plentiful during the period between World War I and II as they were after the War. There were manger scenes, skating ponds and Santa Clauses, but not the huge selection that we have today. There were lots of bunnies, chicks, and black cats and some skeletons. It is doubtful that all of them actually were made for Easter and Halloween, but they are certainly appropriate.

Bunnies and Chicks

Plate 504. (a) Artist bunny mustard pot in multicolored shiny glazes, 3", Black Mark #1, $20.00-30.00. (b) Chick mustard pot (shown in the Fall 1931 Sears catalog for 19¢ with spoon) in blue and white lustre, 3", Red Mark #25, $15.00-25.00.

Plate 505. (a) Girl bunny egg cup in orange lustre with multicolored matte-glazed figure, 3", Red Mark #1, $20.00-30.00. (b) Boy bunnies egg cup in tan lustre with multicolored shiny-glazed figures, 3", Red Mark #15, $20.00-30.00.

Plate 506. (a) Swan egg cup in orange and white lustre, 2½", Black Mark #1, $20.00-30.00. (b) Chick egg cup in yellow and white lustre, 2¼", Black Mark #1, $20.00-30.00.

Plate 507. (a) Bunnies egg cup in teal lustre with multicolored shiny-glazed figures, 2½", Red Mark #1, $20.00-35.00. (b) Pelican egg cup in tan lustre with multicolored shiny-glazed figure, $20.00-30.00.

Plate 508. (a) Cheeping chick egg cup in tan and white lustre, 2½", Black Mark #1, $20.00-30.00. (b) Bunny egg cup in tan lustre with white shiny-glazed figure, 2", Mark obliterated, $20.00-30.00.

Plate 509. (a) Goose egg cup in multicolored matte glazes, 2½", Red Mark #1, $20.00-30.00. (b) Chick egg cup in yellow lustre, 2¼", Red Mark #2, $20.00-30.00.

Plate 510. Chick egg cup in tan lustre, 2½", Black Mark #1, $20.00-30.00.

Plate 511. (a) Bug-eyed bunny cache pot in multicolored matte glazes, 4", $18.00-28.00. (b) Bug-eyed bunny cache pot in tan lustre with multicolored matte glazes, 3¾", $18.00-28.00. (Both are unmarked, but the same pieces with slightly different glazes from another collection have Black Mark #1.)

Plate 512. (a) Bunny cache pot in multicolored lustre glazes, 3½", Red Mark #2, $18.00-28.00. (b) Bunny cache pot in yellow and tan lustre, 3¼", Black Mark #1, $18.00-28.00.

Plate 513. (a) Bunny figurine in white lustre, 2", Black Mark #38, $7.00-12.00. (b) Bunny on egg figurine in multicolored matte glazes, 4¼", Red Mark #16, $15.00-22.00. (c) Bunny cache pot in multicolored lustre glazes, 2½", Black Mark #1, $18.00-28.00.

Plate 514.(a) Bisque bunny figurine, 3¼", Black Mark #1, $10.00-15.00. (b) Rare Easter basket bunny in yellow lustre with multicolored shiny glazes, Red Mark #21, $30.00-45.00 if complete with reed handle.

Black Cats and Skeletons

Plate 515. (a) Black cat on orange matte-glazed pincushion, 3", Black Mark #1, $28.00-38.00. (b) Black cat with blue lustre nut cup, 2", Made In Occupied Japan, $20.00-30.00.

Plate 516. Cat ashtray in orange and black shiny glazes, 3½", Black Mark #1, $20.00-35.00.

Plate 517. (a) Grim Reaper decanter, 7" inscribed "Poison," with skull cups, all Black Mark #19, $95.00-155.00 set. (b) Skeleton card suit ashtray in bisque with tan lustre, 3½", Black Mark #1 and Blind Mark #1, $25.00-35.00.

Plate 518. (a and c) Pair of bisque skeleton on book candlesticks, 2½", Black Mark #1, $35.00-55.00 pair. (b) Nodder bisque skeleton on book candlestick (jaw is wired and moves up and down), 3¾", Black Mark #1, $75.00-100.00.

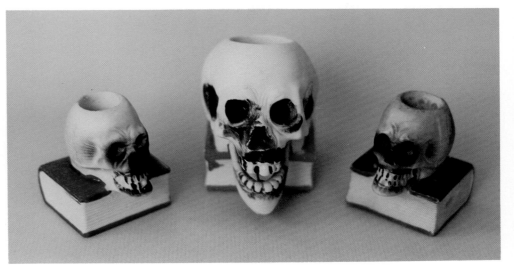

Christmas Items of the 1950's and 60's

Plate 519. Boxed set of eight Christmas place card holders in red and white shiny glazes, 2". One is not marked, six have Black Mark #2, one has Paper Label #39. Box is inscribed "Christmas Card Place Settings, A Commodore Original, No. 3010, 8 Pcs Set, Made In Japan." Set $35.00-50.00.

Plate 520. Christmas angel candlestick in red and white shiny glazes, 4", Paper Label #61 with "© 1958 Holt Howard," $12.00-22.00.

Plate 521. Gold metallic-glazed musical angels, 5½", Black Mark #1, set $25.00-35.00.

Plate 522. (a) Accordion angel in white shiny glaze, 3", Black Mark #8, $15.00-20.00. (b) Candy cane angel bell in multicolored shiny glazes, 4¼", Paper Label with "1956, Napco, Hand Painted Made In Japan," $15.00-22.00.

Plate 523. Three Norcrest China Christmas candlesticks in red and white shiny glazes (came in sets of two identical angels), 3½", Red Metallic Paper Label Made In Japan, $15.00-20.00 each.

Plate 524. Four Norcrest China Christmas angels in red and white shiny glazes. (a, b, d) 3¾". (c) 4" with "real" hair. All Red Metallic Paper Label Made In Japan, $15.00-20.00 each.

Plate 525. (a and c) Pair of Norcrest China Christmas angels in red and white shiny glazes with "real" hair, Red Metallic Paper Label Made In Japan, $15.00-20.00 each. (b) Norcrest China Music Box angel in red and white shiny glazes, 5½", Red Metallic Paper Label Made In Japan, $25.00-40.00.

⚐ Dishes ⚐

The Japanese exported a lot of dishes! Tea sets, demitasse sets, mayonnaise sets, salt and pepper sets. . . the list goes on and on up to and including kitchenware.

Plate 526. Demitasse set in tan and multicolored lustres. Pot is 8¼" tall, all with Black Mark #1, $68.00-78.00 as pictured; $135.00-165.00 for complete set with coffee pot, cream, sugar, and four or six cups and saucers.

Plate 527. Demitasse set in tan and multicolored lustres. Pot is 7¾" tall, all with Black Mark #1, $68.00-78.00 as pictured; $135.00-165.00 for complete set with coffee pot, creamer, sugar, and four or six cups and saucers.

Plate 528. Cherry blossom tea set in gold and white lustre with pink blossoms. Teapot 4¼" no Mark, plate 7¼", Black Mark #1, $55.00-65.00 as pictured; $105.00-150.00 for complete set with teapot, cream, sugar, and six cups, saucers, and plates.

Plate 529. Tea set in blue and tan lustre. Teapot 4¾", Red Mark #1. $55.00-65.00 as pictured; $105.00-150.00 for complete set with teapot, cream, sugar, and six cups, saucers, and plates.

Plate 530. Tea set in white lustre with multicolored bird motif. Pot is 6½" tall, Black Mark #1, (a pre-WWII set from the Akiyama store), $55.00-65.00 as pictured; $125.00-155.00 for complete set with teapot, cream, sugar, and six cups, saucers, and plates.

Plate 531. Hand Painted Nippon tea set in black and white lustre with white birds and multicolored motif, the older original on the same blank as the set in Plate #530. Pot is 6½" tall. $65.00-75.00 as pictured; $205.00-230.00 for complete set with teapot, cream, sugar, and six cups, saucers and plates.

Plate 532. Elephant teapot in blue lustre with multicolored motif, 6¾", Black Mark #43, $55.00-85.00.

Plate 533. Grape teapot in white and gold glazes, 6½" (a pre-WW II piece from the owner's family), Gold Mark #1, $30.00-48.00.

Plate 534. Teapot in blue and white lustre with multicolored floral motif, 6½", Red Mark #3, $35.00-50.00.

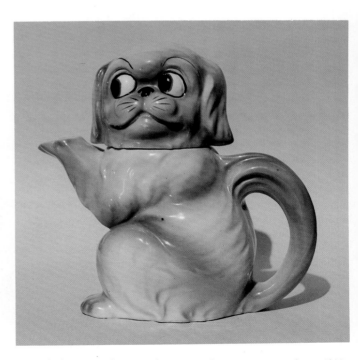

Plate 535. Rare Pekingese dog teapot in green matte glaze, 6¾", Black Mark #1, $150.00-175.00.

Plate 536. Teapot in opal lustre with silver trim, 5½", Black Mark #1, $30.00-48.00.

Plate 537. Teapot in cream and multicolored matte glazes (a pre-WW II piece from the Akiyama store), 5¾", Brown Mark #1, $76.00-151.00.

Plate 538. Chocolate pot in multicolored matte glazes, 8½", Black Mark #1, $36.00-56.00.

Plate 539. Rare mother duck tray with two duckling pitchers in yellow and multicolored lustres, 7½" wide, all with Red Mark #52, $75.00-125.00 set. (This looks like a "marriage," but it is not. The same mark is on all three pieces, and it is not that common a backstamp. The pitchers are curved to fit the tray, and the lid fits perfectly.)

Plate 548. Cream and sugar in blue and tan lustre, 4", Black Mark #1, $22.00-36.00 set.

Plate 549. Cream and sugar in cream matte glaze with multicolored flowers, 4½", Black Mark #22, $36.00-45.00 set.

Plate 550. Celery bowl and six salts with cherry motif in multicolored matte glazes, 11½" wide, bowl Red Mark #67 (salts not marked), $55.00-85.00 set.

Plate 551. Master nut bowl and six nut cups with grape motif in multicolored matte glazes, 6½" wide, bowl Red Mark #67 (nut cups not marked), $55.00-85.00 set.

Plate 552. Ice cream set in green lustre with multicolored bird motif (a pre-WW II set from the Akiyama store), tray 11", plates 6¼", Black Mark #63, $45.00-65.00 set.

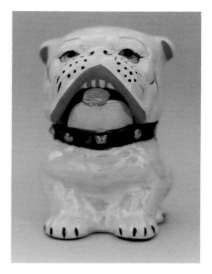

Plate 553. Rare dog marmalade set (ladle is tongue) in white lustre (shown in the Spring 1932 Sears catalog, under the brand name Taisho Ware, with an underplate, in assorted colors, 19¢ per set) 5", Black Mark #1, $95.00-150.00.

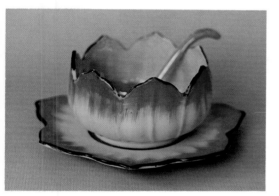

Plate 554. Lotus mayonnaise set in white lustre with yellow and orange matte glazes (shown in the Spring 1928 Sears catalog for $1.19 per set), plate 6¾" diameter, Blue Mark #52, $30.00-45.00 set.

Plate 555. Mayonnaise or sauce bowl in tan lustre with blue lustre ladle, 4¼", Red Mark #1, $35.00-55.00 set. Blue lustre hexagonal tray, 5½", Black Mark #36, $10.00-15.00.

Plate 556. Mayonnaise set in green and opal lustre with multicolored floral motif, 3½", Black Mark #28, $40.00-75.00.

Plate 565. Serving bowl in tan and blue lustre, 8¼" wide and 2¾" deep, Red and Green Mark #64, $25.00-30.00.

Plate 566. Lemon server in multicolored matte glazes, 6¾" diameter, Red Mark #1, $25.00-35.00.

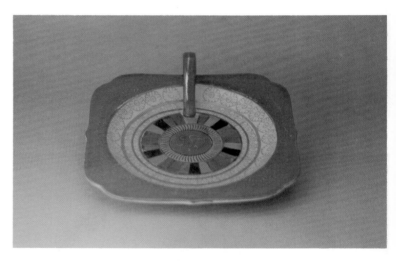

Plate 567. Lemon server in multicolored shiny glazes, 6½" diagonal, Red Mark #1, $25.00-35.00.

Plate 568. (a) Marmalade set with cream matte glaze, 4½" tall, Black Mark #35, $25.00-45.00 set. (b) Covered butter dish with cream matte glaze, 6½" wide, $32.00-65.00.

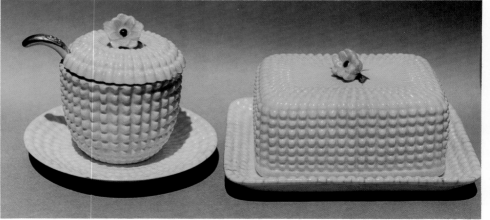

Plate 569. (a) Hexagonal canister in cream crackle glaze with multicolored flowers, 4¾" tall, Black Mark #25, $22.00-32.00. (b) Hexagonal canister in cream crackle glaze with red berries, 4" tall, Black Mark #1, $22.00-32.00.

Plate 570. Canister in cream crackle glaze with yellow floral motif, 4½" tall, Black Mark #24, $22.00-32.00.

Plate 571. (a) Green matte-glazed vessel, 2¾", Black Mark #17, $6.00-12.00. (Write if you know for sure what it is!) (b) Canister in green matte glaze, 4", no Mark, $12.00-22.00. (c) Custard cup in green matte glaze, 2½", Black Mark #1, $9.00-13.00.

Children's Dishes

Plate 580. Children's teapot, creamer and sugar in blue and tan lustre, pot is 4" tall, all Red Mark #1, $35.00-55.00 as pictured, $175.00-250.00 for complete set with four cups, saucers and plates.

Plate 581. Children's tea set pieces in cream matte glaze with multicolored flowers (a mid-1950's set from the owner's family), pot is 4½" tall, Green Mark #1. $58.00-78.00 as pictured; $175.00-250.00 for complete set with teapot, cream and sugar, covered vegetable and four cups, saucers and plates.

Plate 582. A rare and very special elephant figural children's tea set in tan lustre with original box. (A Christmas gift to the owner in 1929. It was purchased for $1.00 before the stock market crash in October of that year, so she had a happy Christmas. It is still in mint condition.) Red Mark #1, $280.00-380.00 complete with four plates, four cups and saucers, creamer, sugar, and teapot.

Plate 583. Figural elephant pitcher in green crackle glaze. The trunk is the handle, and the lid is the tusks and tongue. 8", no Mark. (Another collector has the same pitcher in a different color with Black Mark #1.) $56.00-70.00.

Plate 584. Figural dog pitcher in multicolored shiny glazes, label inscribed "Souvenir of Splitrock Lighthouse," 6½", Green Mark #2, $38.00-50.00.

Plate 585. Seated man with dog handle pitcher in multicolored shiny glazes, Green Mark #68, $45.00-60.00.

Plate 586. Horse and giraffe pitchers in multicolored shiny glazes, 4", both Black Mark #4, $20.00-35.00 each.

Plate 601. (a) Bird condiment set in yellow, white, and brown matte glazes, 4¼" tall, Blue Mark #57, $45.00-85.00. (b) Dog condiment set (tongue is ladle) in tan and white lustre, 3¾" tall, Black Mark #1, $35.00-65.00.

Plate 602. (a) Rabbit condiment set (ears are salts) in tan and blue lustre, 4½" tall, Red Mark #1, $45.00-85.00. (b) A German prototype. Rabbit trio condiment set in tan lustre, 3¾" tall, Marked Germany, $45.00-85.00.

Plate 603. (a) Indian condiment set in multicolored matte glazes, 4" tall, base Black Mark #1, other pieces unmarked, $45.00-85.00. (b) Another German prototype. Camel condiment set in multicolored matte glazes, 2½" tall, Marked Germany, $60.00-95.00.

Plate 604. (a) Three Wise Monkeys condiment set in blue lustre inscribed "Coney Island," 2¾" tall, Black Mark #1 on mustard and tray, salt and pepper have no Mark, $45.00-85.00. (b) Swan and birds condiment set in blue and multicolored lustre, 4¾" long, Black Mark #1 on base, other pieces unmarked, $45.00-85.00.

Plate 605. Dog condiment set in tan and white lustre, 4" tall, no Mark, $45.00-85.00.

Plate 606. Scottie condiment set in orange matte glaze (shown in the Fall 1931 Sears catalog for 65¢), 4", Red Mark #24 on mustard and tray, Red Mark #2 on salt and pepper, $45.00-85.00.

Plate 607. Spotted dog condiment set on tray in tan and blue lustre, tongue is ladle (shown in the Spring 1928 Sears catalog for 85¢), 3", Black Mark #56, $45.00-85.00.

Plate 608. Spotted dog condiment set (all pieces attached) in tan lustre, 4", Black Mark #1, $45.00-85.00.

Plate 609. Condiment set in blue and tan lustre with birds and flowers (a pre-WW II piece from the owner's family), tray is 7¼" diameter, Black Mark #1, $65.00-125.00.

Plate 610. Condiment set on tray in tan lustre with cherry blossoms, tray 5" diameter, tray and pot Black Mark #1, salt and pepper Black Mark #2, $30.00-45.00.

Plate 611. Condiment set on tray in blue lustre with cherry blossoms (shown in the Fall 1927 Sears Catalog for 85¢. By the Fall 1932 catalog it had been reduced to 39¢), 7" long, pot and tray Red Mark #25, salt and pepper Red Mark #2, $38.00-52.00.

Plate 612. Condiment set in tan and blue lustre (shown in the Fall 1929 Sears catalog for $1.00. It is nearly identical to Noritake sets), tray 5¼" wide, Black Mark #1, $30.00-65.00.

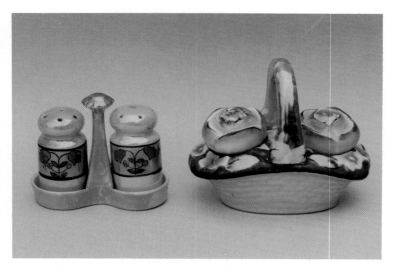

Plate 613. (a) Salt and pepper set on tray in orange, tan, and blue lustre, tray, 2¾" tall; tray Brown Mark #1; salt, Red Mark #1; pepper, Red Mark #2, $15.00-25.00 set. (b) Flower basket salt and pepper in tan lustre with blue and multicolored shiny glazes, 3½" tall, Red Mark #67, $20.00-25.00 set.

Plate 614. (a) Flower basket salt and pepper in yellow lustre with orange matte glaze, 3" tall, Black Mark #1, $20.00-25.00 set. (b) Flower basket salt and pepper in teal and multicolored lustres, 2¼", Red Mark #2, $20.00-25.00 set.

⚐ Post-World War II Collectibles ⚐

We've looked at the older pre-World War II pieces from Japan, so now let's look at some trends in "new" ceramic collectibles—that is, if post-World War II items still seem new!

A real up-and-comer in this field is Joséf Originals. Muriel Joséf George began producing Birthday Girls in Arcadia, California, in 1946. In the 1950's, factories in Japan used her originals to cast molds of the Birthday Girls. Later, very similar ones were made in Korea and Taiwan. The copies were sold at much lower prices. To compete, Mrs. George had to move her operation to Japan in 1955.

In addition to the Birthday Girls, there were Christmas items, animals, and many other designs made in Japan by Mrs. George from 1955 through the early 1970's, when production in Japan ceased. The Joséf Originals produced in Arcadia are marked "California" and date from 1946 to 1955. The Made in Japan Joséf lines are all marked "Joséf Originals." They had two types of Joséf Originals labels: Round with curl and small oval. (See Marks #69 and 70.) Some were also incised or stamped with the logo. All were marked JAPAN. Since the 1970's, Joséfs have been made in Taiwan for Applause, Inc. They are still available today. The Joséf Originals in this book are all from Japan.

For more information on Joséf Originals and reproductions, contact Jim and Kaye Whitaker, P.O. Box 475, Lynnwood, WA 98046, (206) 774-6910.

Plate 615. Birthday Girls holding birthstones, 4". (a) July (with original poem "Rubies stand for harmony, And understanding you will be. You are kind as well as clever, And you'll be content forever.") (b) August. (c) September. From Jim and Kaye Whitaker. $23.00-29.00 each.

Plate 616. Birthday Girls holding numerals. (a) 8 years, 4½", $23.00-29.00. (b) 10 years, 5½", $35.00-42.00. (c) 11 years, 5½", $35.00-42.00. From Jim and Kaye Whitaker.

Plate 617. Lipstick dresser dolls. (a) Blue girl, 3½", $38.00-44.00. (b) Lavender angel, 4¾", $45.00-53.00. (c) Lavender girl, 3½", $43.00-50.00. From Jim and Kaye Whitaker.

Plate 618. Lady dolls. (a) Lady with violin, 6¼", $65.00-75.00. (b) Lady with fan, 5½", $65.00-75.00. From Jim and Kaye Whitaker.

Plate 619. Lady dolls. (a) Lady with parasol, 7¾", $125.00-155.00. (b) Lady with dog, 7¼", $125.00-155.00. From Jim and Kaye Whitaker.

Plate 620. Music boxes. (a) Waltzing couple, 5½", $90.00-115.00. (b) Couple with birds, 4¾", $90.00-115.00. From Jim and Kaye Whitaker.

Plate 621. Wee Folks, 4½", $25.00-35.00 each. From Jim and Kaye Whitaker.

Plate 622. Christmas Pixies, 4½", $25.00-35.00 each. From Jim and Kaye Whitaker.

Plate 623. Christmas Dolls, 4½", $32.00-38.00 each. From Jim and Kaye Whitaker.

Plate 624. (a) Elephant, 3", $20.00-27.00. (b) Mice, 2¾", $20.00-27.00 each. From Jim and Kaye Whitaker.

Other Types of Newer Collectibles to Keep Your Eye On

Plate 625. These are another type of collectible birthday figurine from the 1950's and 60's. (a) Angel, 3½", Silver Made In Japan Label, $12.00-18.00. (b) Angel, 4¼", Black Mark #37, $12.00-18.00.

Plate 626. Lady head vases are another very collectible item. This one's outfit is in brown matte and white shiny glazes, 5¾", Mark #7, $60.00-85.00.

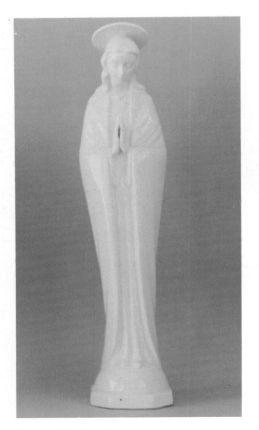

Plate 627. Religious items have grown in popularity as collectibles too. Madonna, 12¾", Paper Label Made In Japan, with "D.C. Floraline," $18.00-24.00.

Plate 628. All sorts of nun and priest figurines were popular in the 50's and 60's, and they, too, have become collectible. Two monk musicians, 5", Paper Label #34 with "© 1964 Inarco, Cleveland, OH," $15.00-22.00 each.

Confusing Figurines

The Chinese and Koreans are exporting figurines and all sorts of ceramics that look a lot like older Japanese ones. Here are some examples, with purchase prices shown, purchased in 1993 at retail stores:

Plate 629. Boy 4¾", Girl 4½", both back-stamped Made In China. $1.00 each.

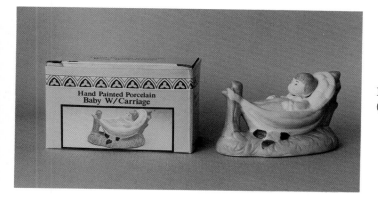

Plate 630. Baby in cradle, 2½", Gold Paper Label Made In China (and the label is already peeling off). $1.00.

Plate 631. Wedding couple, 4¼", backstamped Made In China. $1.00.

Plate 632. This new rabbit looks very modern in design, but the lustre is exactly the same shade as older pieces, so it's included as a glaze example. It is from Korea and retails for $8.99. The pincushion is also new from Korea and retails for $2.49.

Imported Ceramic Novelties 1962 to The Present

As Mr. Bill Naito said, not many ceramics are made in Japan today. Many are from Taiwan, but a trip to a ceramics counter will turn up labels from Korea, Mexico, Thailand, The Philippines, and China as well. It is simply economics. Labor and materials are cheaper in these countries than they are in Japan.

Today's ceramic novelties are usually new designs to keep up with changing tastes, including nostalgia. Lots of new ceramics are Holiday-related. Some Easter and Christmas, with a little Thanksgiving thrown in, used to be all there was. Now there are huge assortments of these three Holidays, plus Halloween, birthday, anniversary, and just about anything else that can be celebrated.

The coffee mug has played an important role in today's ceramics industry. Who hasn't received or given at least one as a gift? Figural salt and peppers have also made a big comeback.

Mr. Naito kindly shared some of his Norcrest catalogs so we could get an idea of what's been made for the past few decades, including the wholesale prices (except for the 1962 catalog, which has retail prices). All of these items are from Asian countries; most are not from Japan.

Selections from the 1962 NAITO Gifts Catalog

Pottery mugs, attractive examples of Japanese folk art 2¼" in distinctive design. AM104, set of 6, boxed, 4.95
Turkish demitasse white porcelain cups and saucers. AL138, set of 6, 4.95

Teakwood tray of heroic proportions . . . 30 x 21" for cocktail parties, buffet suppers, DC105, **$25;** Toma pottery mugs, in folk designs, for every type of beverage. AM101, set of 4, **$4**

Exquisite porcelain: dinner size sugar and creamer, in white, AJ121, **$3 set;** Fluted demitasse cup and saucer, AL136, set of 6, **$4;** chocolate cup and saucer in white, AL140, set of 4, 3.95

Time for tea, and the service is all-important. It calls for this 6-cup white porcelain pot, AK114, **$3 ea.;** white porcelain tea cups to accompany it, 3" size, AL146, set of 4, **1.25**

Miniature screens, 6 panels in gold, with black frame, 14½ x 30", in Scenic or plumtree design, KD111, **$8 ea.**
Bonsai planter, cast iron in rectangular shape, 12" in length. PB108, **$9**

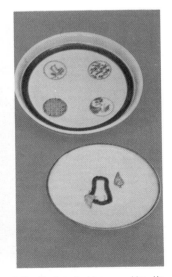

Sukiyaki plate in blue on white. Unusual for table service or for flower arrangement. 9" AL155, **$2 ea.;** dessert plate, blue on white, 6¼" diam. in blue and white. AL156, set of 6, 4.50

Selections From the 1970 Norcrest China Company Catalog

BEEHIVE, BLUEBIRDS AND FONDUE ACCESSORIES PRODUCE FAST TURNOVER

GIVE YOUR HOLIDAY SALES A BOOST WITH NORCREST FIGURINES, SALT AND PEPPER SHAKERS

WHIMSICAL ANIMALS AND COLORFUL PIXIES

(35)

A-500 4 asst. 6.60 dz. pc.   A-144 2 asst. 6.90 dz. pc.   A-529 3 asst. 4.80 dz. pc.   A-766 3 asst. 3.00 dz. pc.   A-381 2 asst. 13.50 dz. pc.

A-33 6 asst. 7.20 dz. pc.   A-34 6 asst. 7.20   A-112 6 asst. 7.20 dz. pc.   A-113 6 asst. 7.20 dz. pc.   A-626 3 asst. 3.90 dz. pc.

DB-27 2 asst. 3.00 dz. pc.   DB-28 2 asst. 3.00 dz. pc.   DB-29 2 asst. 1.80 dz. pc.   DB-30 2.10   A-466 3 asst. 4.50 dz. pc.   A-612 3 asst. 4.20 dz. pc.   A-528 3 asst. 2.70 dz. pc.

F-80 4 asst. 3.60 dz. pc.   F-123 4 asst. 4.20 dz. pc.   F-150 3 asst. 4.20 dz. pc.   F-154 3 asst. 5.40 dz. pc.   F-157 3 asst. 4.20 dz. pc.   A-627 3 asst. 4.80 dz. pc.

F-186 3 asst. 4.20 dz. pc.   F-187 3 asst. 4.50 dz. pc.   F-208 3 asst. 4.50 dz. pc.   F-225 3 asst. 4.50 dz. pc.   F-240 3 asst. 6.00 dz. pc.   F-417 6 asst. 5.40 dz. pc.

F-466 4 asst. 5.40 dz. pc.   F-705 6 asst. 3.00 dz. pc.   F-786 4 asst. 3.00 dz. pc.   F-807 4 asst. 3.00 dz. pc.

LITTLE ALPINE FOLKS, BLOOMER GIRLS, MERMAIDS AND BABY FIGURINES

F-79 2 asst. 10.80 dz. pc.   F-86 2 asst. 10.80 dz. pc.   F-87 2 asst. 10.80 dz. pc.   F-101 2 asst. 10.80 dz. pc.   F-102 4 asst. 10.80 dz. pc.   F-103 2 asst. 10.80 dz. pc.

F-242 4 asst. 8.40 dz. pc.   F-163 2 asst. 6.60 dz. pc.   F-169 2 asst. 8.40 dz. pc.   F-260 3 asst. 8.40 dz. pc.   F-271 2 asst. 7.80 dz. pc.   F-272 3 asst. 7.50 dz. pc.   F-270 2 asst. 15.00 dz. pc.

F-140 6 asst. 6.00 dz. pc.   F-158 6 asst. 6.00 dz. pc.   M-287 9.00 per st.   F-189 3 asst. 4.50 dz. pc.   F-295 3 asst. 3.00 dz. pc.   F-162 3 asst. 6.00 dz. pc.

F-209 4 ast. 6.60 dz. pc.   F-287 2 asst. 10.80 dz. pc.   F-288 2 asst. 9.60 dz. pc.   F-289 2 asst. 9.60 dz. pc.   F-290 3 asst. 8.40 dz. pc.   F-291 3 asst. 9.80 dz. pc.

F-85 3 asst. 7.80 dz. pc.   F-114 6 asst. 7.20 dz. pc.   F-219 3 asst. 4.20 dz. pc.   F-229 3 asst. 3.60 dz. pc.   F-298 3 asst. 5.40 dz. pc.   F-299 3 asst. 6.00 dz. pc.   F-812 3 asst. 5.40 dz. pc.

HAPPINESS IS A FAST SELLING NORCREST COOKIE JAR

COLORFUL COOKIE JARS TO GLADDEN THE HEARTS OF THE COOKIE GENERATION

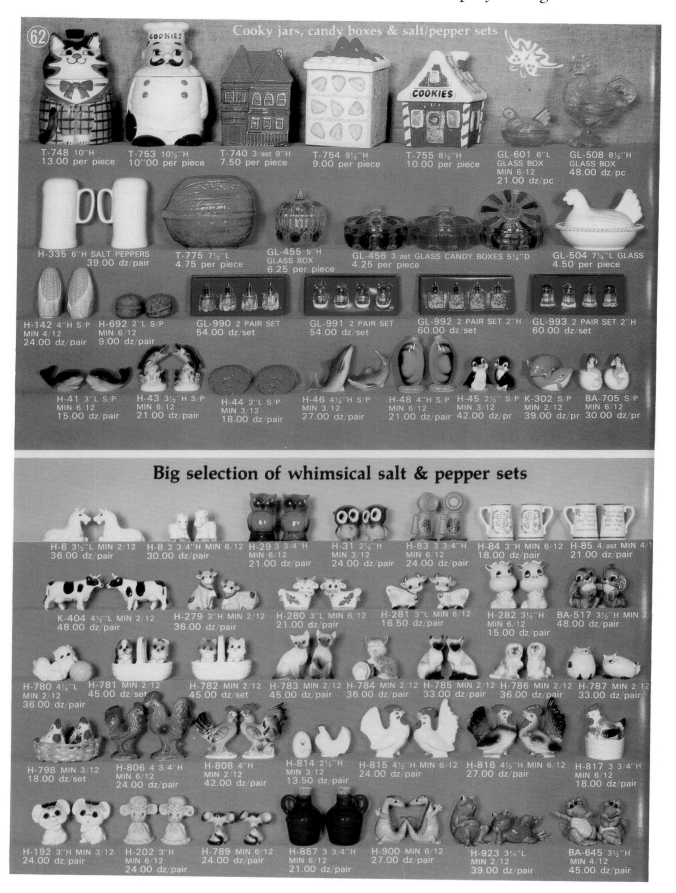

Cooky jars, candy boxes & salt/pepper sets

(62)

T-748 10"H
13.00 per piece

T-753 10½"H
10"00 per piece

T-740 3/ast 9"H
7.50 per piece

T-754 9½"H
9.00 per piece

T-755 8½"H
10.00 per piece

GL-601 6"L
GLASS BOX
MIN 6/12
21.00 dz/pc

GL-508 8½"H
GLASS BOX
48.00 dz/pc

H-335 6"H SALT/PEPPERS
39.00 dz/pair

T-775 7½"L
4.75 per piece

GL-455 5"H
GLASS BOX
6.25 per piece

GL-456 3/ast GLASS CANDY BOXES 5¼"D
4.25 per piece

GL-504 7¼"L GLASS
4.50 per piece

H-142 4"H S/P
MIN 4/12
24.00 dz/pair

H-692 2"L S/P
MIN 6/12
9.00 dz/pair

GL-990 2 PAIR SET
54.00 dz/set

GL-991 2 PAIR SET
54.00 dz/set

GL-992 2 PAIR SET 2"H
60.00 dz/set

GL-993 2 PAIR SET 2"H
60.00 dz/set

H-41 3"L S/P
MIN 6/12
15.00 dz/pair

H-43 3½"H S/P
MIN 6/12
21.00 dz/pair

H-44 3"L S/P
MIN 3/12
18.00 dz/pair

H-46 4¼"H S/P
MIN 3/12
27.00 dz/pair

H-48 4"H S/P
MIN 6/12
21.00 dz/pair

H-45 2½" S/P
MIN 3/12
42.00 dz/pr

K-302 S/P
MIN 2/12
39.00 dz/pr

BA-705 S/P
MIN 6/12
30.00 dz/pr

Big selection of whimsical salt & pepper sets

H-6 3½"L MIN 2/12
36.00 dz/pair

H-8 2 3/4"H MIN 6/12
30.00 dz/pair

H-29 3 3/4"H
MIN 6/12
21.00 dz/pair

H-31 2½"H
MIN 3/12
24.00 dz/pair

H-83 3 3/4"H
MIN 6/12
24.00 dz/pair

H-84 3"H MIN 6/12
18.00 dz/pair

H-85 4/ast MIN 4/1
21.00 dz/pair

K-404 4½"L MIN 2/12
48.00 dz/pair

H-279 3"H MIN 2/12
36.00 dz/pair

H-280 3"L MIN 6/12
21.00 dz/pair

H-281 3"L MIN 6/12
16.50 dz/pair

H-282 3½"H
MIN 6/12
15.00 dz/pair

BA-517 3½"H MIN 2/
48.00 dz/pair

H-780 4¼"L
MIN 2/12
36.00 dz/pair

H-781 MIN 2/12
45.00 dz/set

H-782 MIN 2/12
45.00 dz/set

H-783 MIN 2/12
45.00 dz/pair

H-784 MIN 2/12
36.00 dz/pair

H-785 MIN 2/12
33.00 dz/pair

H-786 MIN 2/12
36.00 dz/pair

H-787 MIN 2/12
33.00 dz/pair

H-798 MIN 3/12
18.00 dz/set

H-806 4 3/4"H
MIN 6/12
24.00 dz/pair

H-808 4"H
MIN 2/12
42.00 dz/pair

H-814 2½"H
MIN 3/12
13.50 dz/pair

H-815 4½"H MIN 6/12
24.00 dz/pair

H-816 4½"H MIN 6/12
27.00 dz/pair

H-817 3 3/4"H
MIN 6/12
18.00 dz/pair

H-192 3"H MIN 3/12
24.00 dz/pair

H-202 3"H
MIN 6/12
24.00 dz/pair

H-789 MIN 6/12
24.00 dz/pair

H-887 3 3/4"H
MIN 6/12
21.00 dz/pair

H-900 MIN 6/12
27.00 dz/pair

H-923 3½"L
MIN 2/12
39.00 dz/pair

BA-645 3½"H
MIN 4/12
45.00 dz/pair

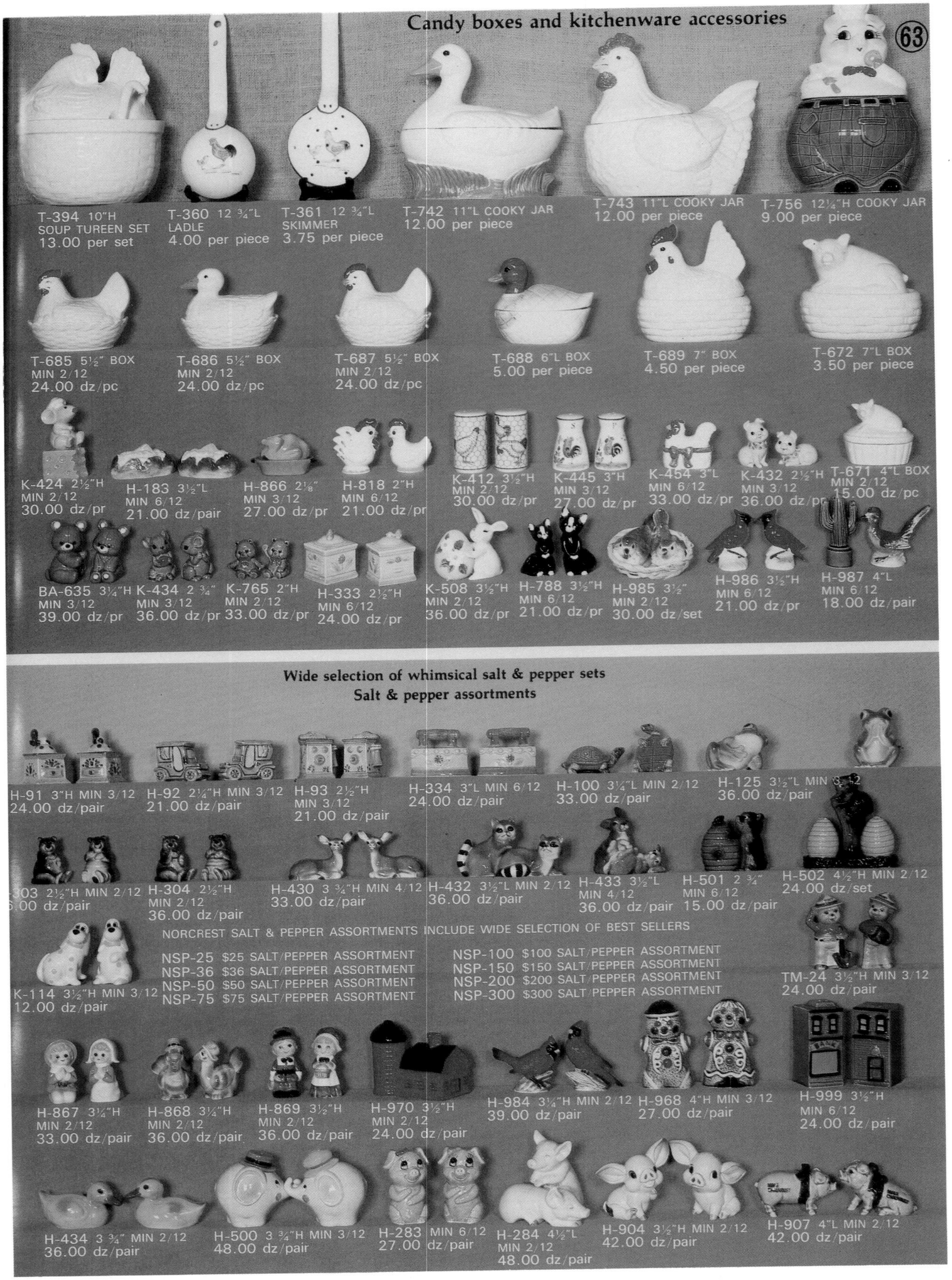

Candy boxes and kitchenware accessories

63

T-394 10"H
SOUP TUREEN SET
13.00 per set

T-360 12 ¾"L
LADLE
4.00 per piece

T-361 12 ¾"L
SKIMMER
3.75 per piece

T-742 11"L COOKY JAR
12.00 per piece

T-743 11"L COOKY JAR
12.00 per piece

T-756 12¼"H COOKY JAR
9.00 per piece

T-685 5½" BOX
MIN 2/12
24.00 dz/pc

T-686 5½" BOX
MIN 2/12
24.00 dz/pc

T-687 5½" BOX
MIN 2/12
24.00 dz/pc

T-688 6"L BOX
5.00 per piece

T-689 7" BOX
4.50 per piece

T-672 7"L BOX
3.50 per piece

K-424 2½"H
MIN 2/12
30.00 dz/pr

H-183 3½"L
MIN 6/12
21.00 dz/pair

H-866 2⅛"
MIN 3/12
27.00 dz/pr

H-818 2"H
MIN 6/12
21.00 dz/pr

K-412 3½"H
MIN 2/12
30.00 dz/pr

K-445 3"H
MIN 3/12
27.00 dz/pr

K-454 3"L
MIN 6/12
33.00 dz/pr

K-432 2½"H
MIN 3/12
36.00 dz/pr

T-671 4"L BOX
MIN 2/12
15.00 dz/pc

BA-635 3¼"H
MIN 3/12
39.00 dz/pr

K-434 2 ¾"
MIN 3/12
36.00 dz/pr

K-765 2"H
MIN 2/12
33.00 dz/pr

H-333 2½"H
MIN 6/12
24.00 dz/pr

K-508 3½"H
MIN 2/12
36.00 dz/pr

H-788 3½"H
MIN 6/12
21.00 dz/pr

H-985 3½"
MIN 2/12
30.00 dz/set

H-986 3½"H
MIN 6/12
21.00 dz/pr

H-987 4"L
MIN 6/12
18.00 dz/pair

Wide selection of whimsical salt & pepper sets
Salt & pepper assortments

H-91 3"H MIN 3/12
24.00 dz/pair

H-92 2¼"H MIN 3/12
21.00 dz/pair

H-93 2½"H
MIN 3/12
21.00 dz/pair

H-334 3"L MIN 6/12
24.00 dz/pair

H-100 3¼"L MIN 2/12
33.00 dz/pair

H-125 3½"L MIN 3/12
36.00 dz/pair

H-303 2½"H MIN 2/12
6.00 dz/pair

H-304 2½"H
MIN 2/12
36.00 dz/pair

H-430 3 ¾"H MIN 4/12
33.00 dz/pair

H-432 3½"L MIN 2/12
36.00 dz/pair

H-433 3½"L
MIN 4/12
36.00 dz/pair

H-501 2 ¾"
MIN 6/12
15.00 dz/pair

H-502 4½"H MIN 2/12
24.00 dz/set

NORCREST SALT & PEPPER ASSORTMENTS INCLUDE WIDE SELECTION OF BEST SELLERS

NSP-25 $25 SALT/PEPPER ASSORTMENT
NSP-36 $36 SALT/PEPPER ASSORTMENT
NSP-50 $50 SALT/PEPPER ASSORTMENT
NSP-75 $75 SALT/PEPPER ASSORTMENT

NSP-100 $100 SALT/PEPPER ASSORTMENT
NSP-150 $150 SALT/PEPPER ASSORTMENT
NSP-200 $200 SALT/PEPPER ASSORTMENT
NSP-300 $300 SALT/PEPPER ASSORTMENT

K-114 3½"H MIN 3/12
12.00 dz/pair

TM-24 3½"H MIN 3/12
24.00 dz/pair

H-867 3¼"H
MIN 2/12
33.00 dz/pair

H-868 3¼"H
MIN 2/12
36.00 dz/pair

H-869 3½"H
MIN 2/12
36.00 dz/pair

H-970 3½"H
MIN 2/12
24.00 dz/pair

H-984 3¼"H MIN 2/12
39.00 dz/pair

H-968 4"H MIN 3/12
27.00 dz/pair

H-999 3½"H
MIN 6/12
24.00 dz/pair

H-434 3 ¾" MIN 2/12
36.00 dz/pair

H-500 3 ¾"H MIN 3/12
48.00 dz/pair

H-283 MIN 6/12
27.00 dz/pair

H-284 4½"L
MIN 2/12
48.00 dz/pair

H-904 3½"H MIN 2/12
42.00 dz/pair

H-907 4"L MIN 2/12
42.00 dz/pair

CHARMING KITCHEN & TABLEWARE ACCESSORIES (64)

T-812 5"D BUTTER TUB MIN 2/12 45.00 dz/pc

GL-518 4"D GLASS BUTTERDISH MIN 2/12 18.00 dz/pc

GL-507 5"L GLASS CANDY BOX MIN 2/12 27.00

D-86 6/ast 5"D BONBON DISH MININUM 6/12 24.00 dz/pc

TM-50 7"L TEAPOT 72.00 dz/pc

K-105 7"L TEAPOT 72.00 dz/pc

T-821 5½" CREAMER MIN 4/12 18.00 dz/pc

T-814 5½" CREAMER MIN 2/12 21.00 dz/pc

K-425 4½"H CHEESESHAKER MIN 4/12 33.00 dz/pc

T-802 4"H NAPKINHOLDER MIN 8/12 27.00 dz/pc

H-968 4" MIN 2/12 SALT PEPPER 27.00 dz/peir

TM-51 4½" SUG/CRM 66.00 dz/set

K-107 4½" SUG/CRM 66.00 dz/set

H-279 3"L MIN 2/12 SALT/PEPPER 36.00 dz/pair

H-281 3"L MIN 6/12 SALT/PEPPER 16.50 dz/pair

K-426 6"D CHEESECOVER 63.00 dz/pc

H-503 3 3/4" S/P MIN 6/12 36.00 dz/pc

H-292 4"H S/P MIN 6/12 27.00 dz/pair

TM-56 3¼"H MUG MIN 6/12 36.00 dz/pc

K-106 3¼"H MUG MIN 6/12 36.00 dz/pc

H-280 3"L SALT/PEPPER MIN 6/12 21.00 dz/pair

H-819 8¼"H S/P MIN 6/12 21.00 dz/pair

K-424 S/P MIN 2/12 30.00 dz/pair

K-510 2 3/4" S/P MIN 2/12 45.00 dz/pair

H-387 S/P MIN 2/12 36.00 dz/pc

K-765 S/P MIN 2/12 33.00 dz/pc

H-305 S/P MIN 2/12 30.00 dz/pc

H-306 S/P MIN 2/12 30.00 dz/pr

Butter tubs, cow creamers, salt/peppers & tableware

strawberry & cow designs (65)

K-408 10"L FIGURINE 14.50 per piece

K-403 7 3/4"L MILK PITCHER MIN 4/12 4.50 per piece

K-409 6 3/4"L FIGURINE 6.00 per piece

K-400 6"L FIGURINE MIN 3/12 5.00 per piece

K-401 8" COVERED BUTTERDISH 8.00 per piece

K-406 7"D COVERED CHEESE SERVER 9.50 per piece

K-402 4½"D BUTTER TUB 5.00 per piece

K-404 4½"L SALT & PEPPER MIN 2-12 4.00 per pair

K-405 6 3/4"L CHEESE BOX 4.00 per piece MIN 4/12

Monthly girls & angel figurines 87

SM-133 12/ast ANGELS OF THE MONTH 4" MIN 1 dz 39.00 dz/pc

SM-137 12/ast ANGELS OF THE MONTH 2"H MIN 1 dz 9.60 dz/pc   SM-138 12/ast BABIES OF THE MONTH 2"H MIN 1 dz 8.10 dz/pc

F-703 12/ast FLOWER GIRLS OF THE MONTH 4"H MIN 1 dz 18.00 dz/pc

F-712 12/ast BONNET GIRLS OF THE MONTH 3"H MIN 1 dz 27.00 dz/pc

Monthly girls & angel figurines 86

F-704 12/ast GIRLS OF THE MONTH 4"H MIN 1 dz 42.00 dz/pc

F-701 12/ast BONNET GIRLS OF THE MONTH 2"H MIN 1 dz
8.40 dz/pc   F-735 FLOWER GIRLS OF THE MONTH 2"H MIN 1 dz
9.60 dz/pc

F-705 12/ast ANGELS OF THE MONTHLY 4½"H MIN 1 dz 15.00 dz/pc

F-702 GIRLS OF THE MONTH 3½"H MIN 1 dz 15.00 dz/pc

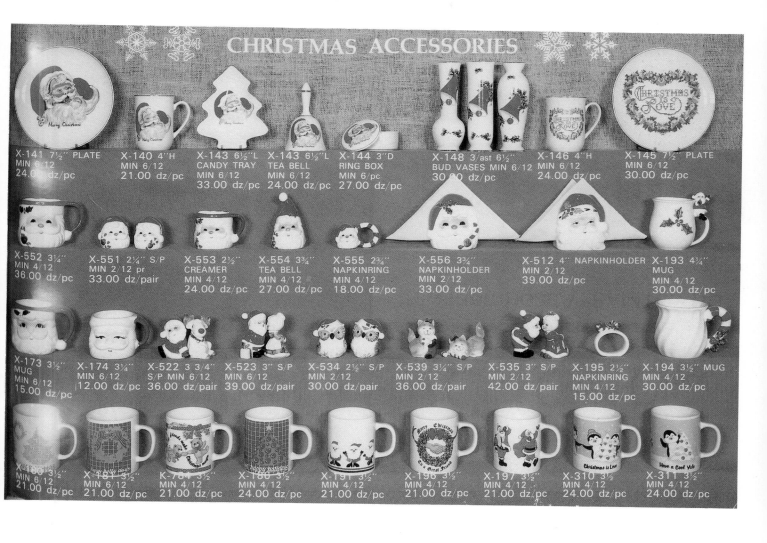

CHRISTMAS ACCESSORIES

X-141 7½'' PLATE
MIN 6/12
24.00 dz/pc

X-140 4''H
MIN 6/12
21.00 dz/pc

X-143 6½''L
CANDY TRAY
MIN 6/12
33.00 dz/pc

X-143 6½''L
TEA BELL
MIN 6/12
24.00 dz/pc

X-144 3''D
RING BOX
MIN 6/pc
27.00 dz/pc

X-148 3/ast 6½''
BUD VASES MIN 6/12
30.00 dz/pc

X-146 4''H
MIN 6/12
24.00 dz/pc

X-145 7½'' PLATE
MIN 6/12
30.00 dz/pc

X-552 3¼''
MIN 4/12
36.00 dz/pc

X-551 2¼'' S/P
MIN 2/12 pr
33.00 dz/pair

X-553 2½''
CREAMER
MIN 4/12
24.00 dz/pc

X-554 3¾''
TEA BELL
MIN 4/12
27.00 dz/pc

X-555 2¾''
NAPKINRING
MIN 4/12
18.00 dz/pc

X-556 3¾''
NAPKINHOLDER
MIN 2/12
33.00 dz/pc

X-512 4'' NAPKINHOLDER
MIN 2/12
39.00 dz/pc

X-193 4¼''
MUG
MIN 4/12
30.00 dz/pc

X-173 3½''
MUG
MIN 6/12
15.00 dz/pc

X-174 3¼''
MIN 6/12
12.00 dz/pc

X-522 3 3/4''
S/P MIN 6/12
36.00 dz/pc

X-523 3'' S/P
MIN 6/12
39.00 dz/pair

X-534 2½'' S/P
MIN 2/12
30.00 dz/pair

X-539 3¼'' S/P
MIN 2/12
36.00 dz/pair

X-535 3'' S/P
MIN 2/12
42.00 dz/pair

X-195 2½''
NAPKINRING
MIN 4/12
15.00 dz/pc

X-194 3½'' MUG
MIN 4/12
30.00 dz/pc

X-180 3½''
MIN 6/12
21.00 dz/pc

X-181 3½''
MIN 6/12
21.00 dz/pc

K-784 3½''
MIN 4/12
21.00 dz/pc

X-186 3½''
MIN 4/12
24.00 dz/pc

X-191 3½''
MIN 4/12
21.00 dz/pc

X-196 3½''
MIN 4/12
21.00 dz/pc

X-197 3½''
MIN 4/12
21.00 dz/pc

X-310 3½''
MIN 4/12
24.00 dz/pc

X-311 3½''
MIN 4/12
24.00 dz/pc

60

HALLOWEEN HAUNTS
From Norcrest

TL–21 WHITE CAT
FIGURINE 8"H
MIN 1/12
42.00 dz/pc

TL–22 BLACK CAT
FIGURINE 8"H
MIN 1/12
42.00 dz/pc

K–233 TEAPOT
7½"H MIN 1/12
15.00 each piece

E–697 VASE
5"H MIN 1/12
6.50 each piece

TJ–632 ELECTRIC
CORD LIGHT
7"H MIN 1/12
7.50 each piece

KT–91 CANDLE LAMP
6"H MIN 1/12
54.00 dz/pc

K–90 PLANTER
6"LG MIN 2/12
63.00 dz/pc

K–91 CANDLEHOLDER ONLY
2½"H MIN 3/12 PAIR
75.00 dz/pair

TK–90 FIGURINES 3/ast
4½"H MIN 3/12
27.00 dz/pc

TK–82 FIGURINES
2/ast 3"H MIN 2/12
PACKED PIX BOX
24.00 dz/pc

KT–90 CANDLE LAMP
4"H MIN 6/12
30.00 dz/pc

K–92 FIGURINES 2/ast
MIN 6/12
33.00 dz/pc

TK–86 MUG OR PLANTER
3½"H MIN
24.00 dz/pc

KC–521 BLACK ONLY MUG
4"H MIN 4/12
15.00 dz/pc

W–91 WOODEN CANDY BASKETS
6/12 3"H MIN 6/12
24.00 dz/pc

T–93 CANDLE LAMP
3½"H MIN 1/12
30.00 dz/pc

HALLOWEEN WITCHES AND PUMPKINS FOR DECORATIVE FUN AND FLAIR

TK–97 HAUNTED HOUSE ORNAMENT

TH–900 SALT + PEPPER
2½"H MIN 1/12
33.00 dz/pair

TK–97 HAUNTED ORNAMENT
5"H MIN 1/12
PACKED IN PIX BOX
27.00 dz/pc

KT–96 FIGURINE
4½"H MIN 1/12
24.00 dz/pc

TK–82 FIGURINES 3/ast
3½"H MIN 3/12
30.00 dz/pc

T–96 FIGURINES 2/ast
3½"H MIN 4/12
39.00 dz/pc

TJ–631 ELECTRIC
CORD LIGHT
6½"H MIN 1/12
7.50 each piece

TK–99 FIGURINES 4/ast
4½"H MIN 4/12
30.00 dz/pc

KJ–724 THIMBLES
2/ast 2"H
MIN 6/12
21.00 dz/pc

TK–83 TEA BELLS 3/ast
4"H MIN 3/12
24.00 dz/pc

TH–621 SALT + PEPPER
2½"H MIN 2/12
33.00 dz/set

TH–90 SALT + PEPPER
2½"H MIN 3/12
24.00 dz/pair

TK–87 NAPKINRING
2"D MIN 6/12
18.00 dz/pc

TK–89 FIGURINES 3/ast
3"H MIN 6/12
24.00 dz/pc

TK–88 VOTIVE CANDLE CUPS
2/ast 3"H MIN 4/12
36.00 dz/pc

T–97 FIGURINES 2/ast
3½"H MIN 4/12
33.00 dz/pc

HALLOWEEN HAUNTS
From Norcrest

61

KT–98 FIGURINE
6"H MIN 4/12
27.00 dz/pc

KT–101 PLANTER + CANDY BOWL
6"LG MIN 2/12
30.00 dz/pc

KT–97 FIGURINES 2/ast
2¼"H MIN 6/12
15.00 dz/pc

W–90 MINIATURE WOODEN CANDY BASKETS 3/ast
3¼"H MIN 6/12
24.00 dz/pc

KT–102 FIGURINE
4"LG MIN 4/12
21.00 dz/pc

KT–103 FIGURINES
4"H MIN 4/12
21.00 dz/pc

KT–104 FIGURINE
4¼"H MIN 4/12
21.00 dz/pc

T–80 FIGURINE
3¼"H MIN 6/12
24.00 dz/pc

T–81 VOTIVE CANDLE CUP
4¼"A LG MIN 6/12
27.00 dz/pc

T–83 FIGURINE
3¼"H MIN 6/12
18.00 dz/pc

T–84 FIGURINE
3¼"LG MIN 6/12
18.00 dz/pc

TK–80 FIGURINES 4/ast
4"H MIN 4/12
24.00 dz/pc

CALL TOLL FREE
1-800-547-6753
OREGON residents call
228-7410

T–85 FIGURINE
4"H MIN 6/12
18.00 dz/pc

T–190 MINI TIN CANDY PAIL
3¼"D MIN 1 dozen
9.00 dz/pc

HALLOWEEN HAUNTS

"HALLOWEEN HAUNTS" ASSORTMENTS
Include wide selection of best selling
halloween accessories.
NHA–100 $100 HALLOWEEN HAUNTS ASSORTMENT
NHA–200 $200 HALLOWEEN HAUNTS ASSORTMENT
NHA–300 $300 HALLOWEEN HAUNTS ASSORTMENT
NHA–400 $400 HALLOWEEN HAUNTS ASSORTMENT

T–191 TIN CANDY BOX
5¼"A MIN 1 dozen
15.00 dz/pc

KC–90 MUG + GIFT BOX
3"H MIN 6/12
21.00 dz/pc

T–192 MINI TIN CANDY BUCKET
3"LG MIN 1 dozen
7.20 dz/pc

KT–105 CANDLE LAMP
4¼"D MIN 4/12
24.00 dz/pc

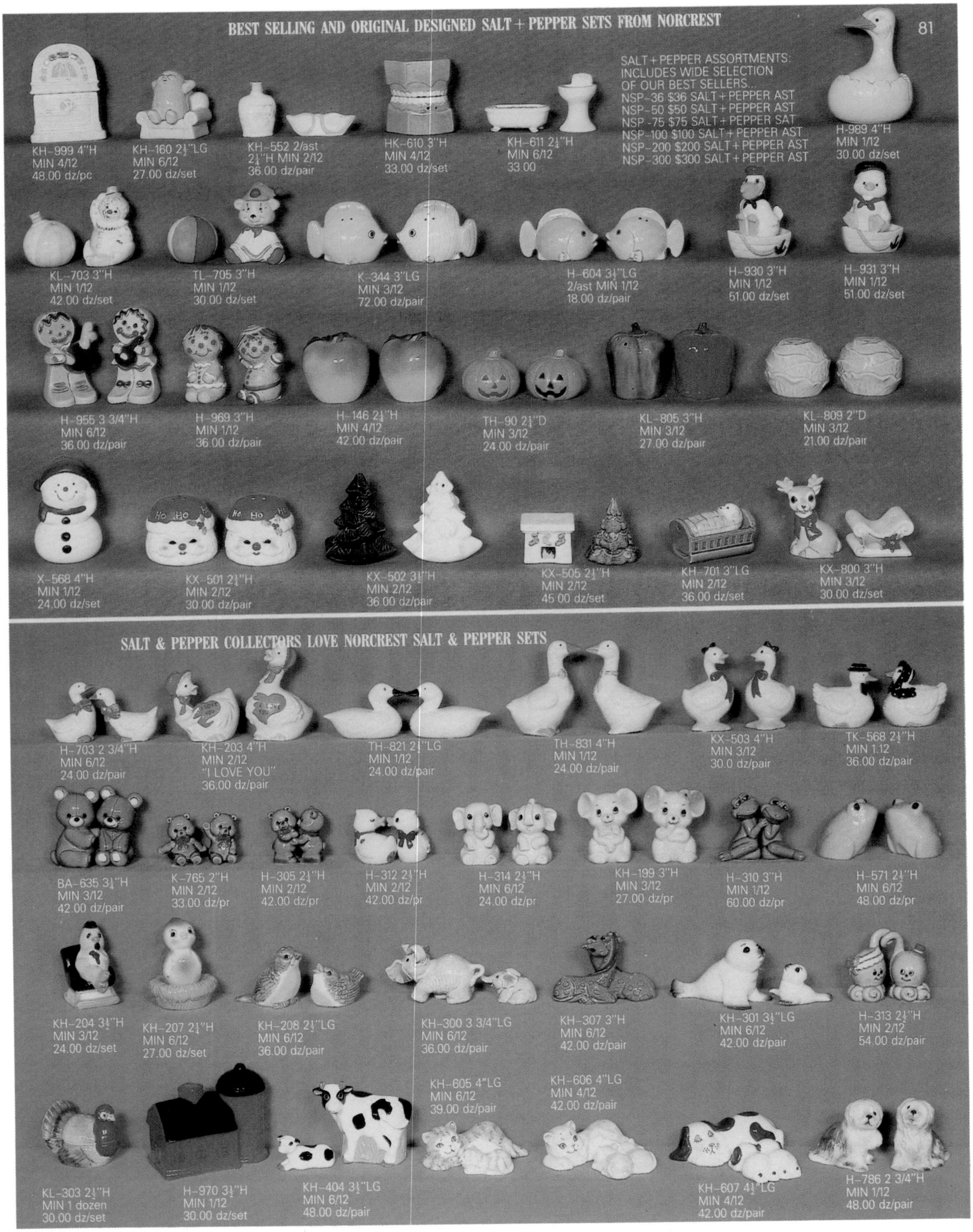
BEST SELLING AND ORIGINAL DESIGNED SALT + PEPPER SETS FROM NORCREST
81
SALT + PEPPER ASSORTMENTS:
INCLUDES WIDE SELECTION
OF OUR BEST SELLERS...
NSP-36 $36 SALT + PEPPER AST
NSP-50 $50 SALT + PEPPER AST
NSP-75 $75 SALT + PEPPER SAT
NSP-100 $100 SALT + PEPPER AST
NSP-200 $200 SALT + PEPPER AST
NSP-300 $300 SALT + PEPPER AST
KH-999 4"H MIN 4/12 48.00 dz/pc
KH-160 2½"LG MIN 6/12 27.00 dz/set
KH-552 2/ast 2¼"H MIN 2/12 36.00 dz/pair
HK-610 3"H MIN 4/12 33.00 dz/set
KH-611 2¼"H MIN 6/12 33.00
H-989 4"H MIN 1/12 30.00 dz/set
KL-703 3"H MIN 1/12 42.00 dz/set
TL-705 3"H MIN 1/12 30.00 dz/set
K-344 3"LG MIN 3/12 72.00 dz/pair
H-604 3½"LG 2/ast MIN 1/12 18.00 dz/pair
H-930 3"H MIN 1/12 51.00 dz/set
H-931 3"H MIN 1/12 51.00 dz/set
H-955 3 3/4"H MIN 6/12 36.00 dz/pair
H-969 3"H MIN 1/12 36.00 dz/pair
H-146 2¼"H MIN 4/12 42.00 dz/pair
TH-90 2¼"D MIN 3/12 24.00 dz/pair
KL-805 3"H MIN 3/12 27.00 dz/pair
KL-809 2"D MIN 3/12 21.00 dz/pair
X-568 4"H MIN 1/12 24.00 dz/set
KX-501 2¼"H MIN 2/12 30.00 dz/pair
KX-502 3½"H MIN 2/12 36.00 dz/pair
KX-505 2¼"H MIN 2/12 45.00 dz/set
KH-701 3"LG MIN 2/12 36.00 dz/set
KX-800 3"H MIN 3/12 30.00 dz/set
SALT & PEPPER COLLECTORS LOVE NORCREST SALT & PEPPER SETS
H-703 2 3/4"H MIN 6/12 24.00 dz/pair
KH-203 4"H MIN 2/12 "I LOVE YOU" 36.00 dz/pair
TH-821 2½"LG MIN 1/12 24.00 dz/pair
TH-831 4"H MIN 1/12 24.00 dz/pair
KX-503 4"H MIN 3/12 30.0 dz/pair
TK-568 2½"H MIN 1.12 36.00 dz/pair
BA-635 3¼"H MIN 3/12 42.00 dz/pair
K-765 2"H MIN 2/12 33.00 dz/pr
H-305 2¼"H MIN 2/12 42.00 dz/pr
H-312 2½"H MIN 2/12 42.00 dz/pr
H-314 2½"H MIN 6/12 24.00 dz/pr
KH-199 3"H MIN 3/12 27.00 dz/pr
H-310 3"H MIN 1/12 60.00 dz/pr
H-571 2½"H MIN 6/12 48.00 dz/pr
KH-204 3½"H MIN 3/12 24.00 dz/set
KH-207 2¼"H MIN 6/12 27.00 dz/set
KH-208 2½"LG MIN 6/12 36.00 dz/pair
KH-300 3 3/4"LG MIN 6/12 36.00 dz/pair
KH-307 3"H MIN 6/12 42.00 dz/pair
KH-301 3½"LG MIN 6/12 42.00 dz/pair
H-313 2½"H MIN 2/12 54.00 dz/pair
KH-605 4"LG MIN 6/12 39.00 dz/pair
KH-606 4"LG MIN 4/12 42.00 dz/pair
KL-303 2½"H MIN 1 dozen 30.00 dz/set
H-970 3½"H MIN 1/12 30.00 dz/set
KH-404 3½"LG MIN 6/12 48.00 dz/pair
KH-607 4½"LG MIN 4/12 42.00 dz/pair
H-786 2 3/4"H MIN 1/12 48.00 dz/pair

86

VINTAGE "BLUE WILLOW" TABLEWARE ACCESSORIES

176–BO PLATTER 12½"LG MIN 4/12
12.00 each piece

177–BO 2/pc ASHTRAY SET
5"D MIN 1/12
11.5 each set

124–BO PLATE 7"D
MIN 6/12
42.00 dz/pc

150–BO PLATE 10½"D
MIN 3/12
10 00 each piece

185–BO SOUP SPOON
5¼"LG MIN 1 dozen
21.00 dz/pc

126–BO PICKLE DISH
4"D MIN 3 dozen
13.50 dz/pc

138–BO
CREAMER
1½"H MIN 6/12
16.50 dz/pc

180–BO
TOOTHPICK
HOLDER
2"H MIN 1 dz
27.00 dz/pc

TC–997 MINIATURE 10/pc
TEA SET 3½"D MIN 1/12
54.00 dz/set

125–BO EGG CUP
2"H MIN 2dz
18.00 dz/pc

137–BO
SALT + PEPPER
3"H MIN 3/12
63.00 dz/pair

187–BO RICE BOWL 7½"D
MIN 3/12
90.00 dz/pc

128–BO RICE BOWL
5"D MIN 1 dozen
33.00 dz/pc

139–BO RING BOX
3½"D MIN 3/12
57.00 dz/pc

174–BO MUG
3¼"H MIN 6/12
33.00 dz/pc

175–BO BUTTERDISH 7"LG
MIN 1/12 11.50 each piece

193–BO SOUP MUG 4¼"D
MIN 6/12 45.00 dz/pc

87

BEST SELLING "BLUE WILLOW" ACCESSORIES

120–BO TEAPOT
9"LG MIN 1/12
16.50 each piece

122–BO COFFEEPOT
7"H MIN 1/12
10.00 each piece

197–BO TEA BELL
5"H MIN 6/12
39.00 dz/pc

173–BO TEAPOT
8¼"LG MIN 1/12
13.00 each piece

170–BO TEAPOT 6"H MIN 1/12
15.00 each piece

123–BO SUGAR + CREAMER SET
5"LG MIN 1/12
9.00 each set

191–BO SUGAR + CREAMER SET
5½"LG MIN 1/12
9.00 each set

171–BO SUGAR + CREAMER SET
3½"D MIN 1/12
9.00 each set

(TOPSIDE) 900–TS RATTAN TEAPOT HANDLES ONLY
7"LG MIN 1 dozen
12.00 dz/pc

121–BO EGGSHELL CUP + SAUCER
WITH GEISHA LADY
5¼"D MIN 1 dozen
54.00 dz/pc

133–BO AFTERDINNER
CUP + SAUCER 4¼"D MIN 1 dz
39.00 dz/pc

134–BO MUG
3¼"H MIN 6/12
36.00 dz/pc

194–BO BEAKER MUG
4¼"H MIN 6/12
39.00 dz/pc

192–BO EGGSHELL CUP + SAUCER
WITH GEISHA LADY
5¼"D MIN 6/12 54.00 dz/pc

Appendix A

Tariff Schedules of the United States Annotated (1963)*

United States Tariff Commission: 1936

Scedule 5. – Nonmetallic and Products
Part 2. – Ceramics Products

For the purposes of the tariff schedules—

(a) a **ceramic article** is a shaped article having glazed or unglazed body of crystalline or substantially crystalline structure, which body is composed essentially of inorganic nonmetallic substances and either is formed from a molten mass which solidifies on cooling, or is formed and subsequently hardened by such heat treatment that the body, if reheated to pyrometric cone 020, would not become more dense, harder, or less porous, but does not include any glass article;

(b) The term **earthenware** embraces ceramic ware, whether or not glazed or decorated, having a fired body which contains clay as an essential ingredient and will absorb more than 3.0 percent of its weight of water;

(c) the term **stoneware** embraces ceramic ware whether or not glazed or decorated, having a body which contains clay as an essential ingredient, is not commonly white, will absorb not more than 3.0 percent of its weight of water, and is naturally opaque (except in very thin pieces) even when fully vitrified;

(d) the term **subporcelain** embraces fine-grained ceramic ware (other than stoneware), whether or not glazed or decorated, having a fired body which is white (unless artificially colored) and will absorb more than 0.5 percent but not more than 3.0 percent of its weight of water;

(e) the terms **chinaware** and **porcelain** embrace fine-grained ceramic ware (other than stoneware), whether or not glazed or decorated, having a body which is white (unless artificially colored) and will not absorb more than 0.5 percent of its weight of water;

(f) the term **bone chinaware** embraces chinaware or porcelain the body of which contains by weight 25 percent or more of calcined bone;

(g) the term **nonbone chinaware** embraces chinaware or porcelain other than bone chinaware; (h) the term "coarse-grained" as applied to ceramicware, embraces such wares having a body made of materials none of which had been washed, ground, or otherwise beneficiated;

(i) the term **fine-grained** as applied to ceramic wares, embraces such wares having a body made of materials any of which had been washed, ground, or otherwise beneficiated; and

(j) the term **body** includes any engobe** or body slip, except engobe or body slip applied to the body as a decoration; and

(k) the water absorption of a ceramic body shall be determined by ASTM test method designated C373-56 (except that test specimens may have a minimum weight of 10 grams, and may have one large surface glazed).

---

*Technical definitions for ceramic types used from 1930 to 1989, (and, to some extent, back to 1909).
**Engobe is another word for slip, a liquid composed of clay particles and water.

Household Table and Kitchen Articles of Earthenware and of China, Porcelain, and Other Vitrified Wares

For tariff purposes pottery is classified under two general categories, namely, (1) earthenware and stoneware, and (2) china and porcelain. Technically, each of these is a different product, but the nomenclature concerning them is not uniform throughout the pottery trade in the United States.

The term "pottery" is often used in this country to describe all pottery articles, regardless of their basic character, and sometimes in a more restrictive sense to designate pottery other than china and porcelain. Again, the terms "chinaware" and "crockery" are often indiscriminately used when referring to all pottery and particularly when referring to table and kitchen articles.

The terms "china" and "porcelain" (considered by many as synonymous) are, however, used technically, and for the most part by the wholesale trade in general, to differentiate from earthenware and stoneware those pottery products composed of a vitrified or vitreous body which is practically impermeable to liquids, and in the finished state more of less translucent. In most countries such vitrified, translucent pottery would be designated porcelain.

It is probable that the term china is used only in English-speaking countries; in the United Kingdom it is used primarily to describe the bone china produced in England; in the United States the term is generally used when referring to English bone china, and with respect to domestic pottery, to designate specifically so-called "Belleek china," and the distinctively American product generally known as "vitreous china."

Although the English and domestic china products here mentioned may often be called porcelain, there are technical and physical differences between such china and true porcelain. The methods of firing glazed china and glazed porcelain, particularly tableware, are different, and usually there is a substantial difference in the character of the glaze applied to the bodies of the respective products.

The bone china produced in England and the Belleek and so-called "vitreous china tableware" (except possibly one-fire ware) produced in the United States are made by the "earthenware" process; that is, the body is first fired at a relatively high temperature which vitrifies it, thereby making it practically impermeable, is then covered with the prepared glaze (usually plumbiferous),[†] and finally subjected to a second fire of considerably lower temperature which vitrifies the glaze and fuses it on the body.

On the other hand, true porcelain is produced by first firing the body at a very low temperature (the resultant product is essentially porous), then covering it with the prepared glaze (usually calcareous[††] or feldspathic[†††]), and subsequently subjecting it to an extremely high temperature which vitrifies the body and glaze, and practically fuses them together.

[†]containing lead
[††]containing calcium carbonate
[†††]containing crystalline minerals

An earthenware body, as distinguished from china or porcelain bodies, is not vitrified, or in some instances may show incipient vitrification. The body is "matured" in the first firing at a relatively high temperature (the resultant product is more or less porous, and permeable), is then covered with the prepared glaze (usually plumbiferous), and subsequently subjected to a second firing at a considerably lower temperature which matures the glaze and fuses it to the body.

In either fire the temperature is not high enough to practically fuse together (as in the case of china or porcelain) the materials of which the body is composed, or (as in the case of true porcelain) the body and the glaze with which it is covered. Earthenware is, therefore, regardless of quality, characteristically more or less porous and absorbent, and except in unusually thin sections, opaque.

The glaze renders it impermeable to liquids and other substances. Unlike true porcelain and the better grades of china, it is susceptible to crazing and to discoloration by grease or other substances where the body has become exposed through cracking or chipping off of the glaze.

The term "earthenware" is often used in this country, in the United Kingdom, and possibly in other countries to designate non-vitrified pottery products. Among other terms used in the more important pottery producing countries are: faience, majolica, white granite, semiporcelain, ironstone china, silicon china, semivitreous china, queensware, cream-colored ware, and flint ware. Most of these terms are generally used to distinguish some specific type of earthenware.

The importance and need of a uniform terminology with respect to the various types or classes of pottery sold in the American markets have been emphasized by the difficulties encountered by domestic producers when it was necessary to so describe earthenware products that those produced by manufacturers operating under the Earthenware Manufacturing Industry Code could be distinguished from those produced by manufacturers operating under the Chinaware and Porcelain Manufacturing Industry Code.

The usual commercial articles of earthenware for household table and kitchen use produced in this country maybe divided into two general classes or groups: (1) those having a carefully prepared and uniform body composed of several different materials, produced under the Chinaware and Porcelain Manufacturing Industry Code, and (2) those composed of a body of clay unmixed with other materials, produced under the Earthenware Manufacturing Industry Code. The products coming within each of these two classifications

are, basically, earthenware, but technically and physically they are appreciably different, and there are substantial differences in their costs of production, articles in the first group having as a whole a higher cost than corresponding articles in the second group.

The Chinaware and Porcelain Manufacturing Industry Code covers two distinct branches of the pottery tableware industry. They are (1) the Vitrified China Branch, which produces a comparatively small amount of vitreous china dinnerware buy whose major product is vitreous china hotel and restaurant ware, and (2) the so-called "white ware" branch, designated the "Semi-Vitrified China Branch" in the code, as amended, whose production is almost wholly earthenware household table and kitchen articles.

No difficulty arises with respect to identification and proper classification of the type of ware produced by manufacturers operating under the vitrified china branch of the industry.

In order, however, to distinguish their earthenware products from those produced by the earthenware manufacturing industry, it was necessary for producers in the white ware branch to fix upon a specific term for the type they produced. The terminology used by that branch of the industry for this purpose is contained in subsection (2), approved December 3, 1934, amending article II, section (a) of the Chinaware and Porcelain Manufacturing Industry Code, which reads in part as follows:

> (2) The term "Semi-Vitrified China Branch" of the industry as used herein is defined to mean the manufacturers of all properly glazed semi-vitreous or semi-vitrified china, tableware, kitchenware, dinnerware, and kindred lines...earthenware, stoneware, or clay flower pots, however, being hereby specifically excluded.

For the purposes of the administration of that code, therefore, the term "earthenware" has been discarded, and the terms "semi-vitreous" or "semivitrified" china have been adopted. For the sake of brevity or to avoid awkward repetition, the term "earthenware" will often be used in this report as equivalent to the terms "semivitreous china" and "semivitrified china." In addition, except where specifically differentiated, the words "china" and "porcelain" will be treated as synonymous terms to distinguish vitrified translucent pottery from earthenware and stoneware. The term "stoneware" is generally used to designate a type of pottery having a vitrified, impermeable, body. The characteristic opacity of the body distinguishes it from china and porcelain, and its impermeability distinguishes it from earthenware. A classification in summary form of the principal types of household table and kitchen articles of pottery sold in the United States is given in the following table.

Principal types of pottery household table and kitchen articles [1]

Tariff paragraph	Body materials	Firing and glaze	Body characteristics	Tariff terminology	Code terminology	Common names
210	Natural clay, unwashed and unmixed.	1 fire, or high first fire; usually lead glaze.	Nonvitrified, absorbent, opaque.	Common earthenware.	Earthenware (earthenware manufacturing industry).	Earthenware.
	Various............	1 fire, salt glaze............	Vitrified, impermeable, opaque.	Common salt glazed stoneware.	Stoneware (subclassification under earthenware manufacturing industry).	Stoneware.
211	Clays mixed with other materials.	High first fire, low second fire (occasionally only 1 fire); usually lead glaze.	Nonvitrified, absorbent, opaque.	Earthenware, including white granite, semiporcelain, cream-colored ware.	Semivitrified or semivitreous china (branch of chinaware and porcelain manufacturing industry).	Earthenware, china, chinaware, semiporcelain, white granite, and white ware.
		1 fire, or high first fire; usually salt glaze or lead glaze.	Vitrified, impermeable, opaque.	Stoneware............	Stoneware (subclassification under earthenware manufacturing industry).	Stoneware.
212	Clays mixed with other materials.	High first fire, low second fire; lead glaze.	Vitrified, impermeable, more or less translucent.	China............	Vitrified or vitreous china (branch of chinaware and porcelain manufacturing industry).	China, porcelain.
		Low first fire, high second fire; usually calcareous or feldspathic glaze.	.....do..............	Porcelain............	(²)............	Porcelain, china.

¹ Crockery is a term often used to designate all pottery, and more specifically kitchen articles.
² Little, if any, produced in the United States.

Appendix B

⚞ Summary of Imported Tableware 1929 – 1934 ⚟

In response to growing concern on the part of American pottery manufacturers due to a decline in sales, the United States Tariff Commission took a survey to determine quantities of imported tableware from 1929 to 1934.

The survey showed that Japanese imports had outstripped those from European countries. In 1929, 32.4% of imported tableware was Japanese; by 1934 their share had risen to 85.2%. However, foreign competition was not the only reason that domestic pottery suffered a loss. Depression glass also greatly affected sales because it could be manufactured and sold for far less money than ceramic tableware, but that's a different story! The survey tracked only dinnerware, not novelties. But to a collector, it is fascinating to see just how much was imported.

TABLE 6.—*Earthenware, stoneware, china, and porcelain household table and kitchen articles: Imports for consumption, from principal sources, 1929–34*

	1929	1930	1931	1932	1933	1934
Quantity (dozens): [1]						
Japan	7,166,047	5,686,538	4,612,928	4,935,226	7,142,264	8,215,860
United Kingdom	1,540,426	1,173,260	893,954	749,714	773,924	742,898
Germany	3,083,567	2,285,402	1,057,494	671,446	584,179	380,341
Czechoslovakia	751,080	501,155	264,854	218,460	127,590	113,309
France	409,500	263,792	75,781	43,411	28,841	29,388
All other countries	927,643	447,178	218,036	145,370	136,177	158,655
Total	13,878,263	10,357,325	7,123,047	6,763,627	8,792,975	9,640,451
Value:						
Japan	$4,486,837	$3,653,934	$1,990,430	$1,145,109	$1,904,244	$3,179,614
United Kingdom	3,086,559	2,458,624	1,482,983	805,025	953,406	1,232,795
Germany	3,600,971	2,766,780	1,279,365	801,234	796,793	629,862
Czechoslovakia	887,111	540,432	274,210	226,458	149,867	161,961
France	844,379	602,571	208,937	104,413	72,414	81,961
All other countries	941,980	600,369	287,117	172,348	176,841	229,970
Total	13,847,837	10,622,710	5,523,042	3,248,587	4,053,565	5,516,163
Unit value: [1]						
Japan	$0.63	$0.64	$0.43	$0.23	$0.27	$0.39
United Kingdom	2.00	2.10	1.66	1.07	1.23	1.66
Germany	1.17	1.21	1.21	1.19	1.36	1.66
Czechoslovakia	1.18	1.08	1.04	1.01	1.17	1.43
France	2.06	2.28	2.76	2.41	2.51	2.79
All other countries	1.02	1.34	1.32	1.19	1.30	1.45
Average	1.00	1.03	.78	.48	.46	.57
Percent of total quantity:						
Japan	51.6	54.9	64.8	73.0	81.2	85.2
United Kingdom	11.1	11.3	12.5	11.1	8.8	7.7
Germany	22.2	22.1	14.8	9.9	6.6	3.9
Czechoslovakia	5.4	4.8	3.7	3.2	1.5	1.2
France	3.0	2.6	1.1	.6	.3	.3
All other countries	6.7	4.3	3.1	2.2	1.6	1.7
Total	100.0	100.0	100.0	100.0	100.0	100.0
Percent of total value:						
Japan	32.4	34.4	36.0	35.3	47.0	57.7
United Kingdom	22.3	23.1	26.8	24.8	23.5	22.3
Germany	26.0	26.0	23.2	24.7	19.6	11.4
Czechoslovakia	6.4	5.1	5.0	6.7	3.7	2.9
France	6.1	5.7	3.8	3.2	1.8	1.5
All other countries	6.8	5.7	5.2	5.3	4.4	4.2
Total	100.0	100.0	100.0	100.0	100.0	100.0

[1] Figures of quantity under the act of 1922 not comparable with those under the act of 1930 because of difference in method of counting number of pieces. The unit values are consequently also not comparable.

Source: Bureau of Foreign and Domestic Commerce, Department of Commerce.

Appendix C

☒ Tariff Acts and Treasury Decisions ☒

The following Acts and Decisions affected marking of all imported goods,
including Made in Japan ceramics.

THE McKINLEY TARIFF (THE TARIFF ACT OF 1890)

Chapter 1244, Section 6. That on and after the first day of March, eighteen hundred and ninety-one, all articles of foreign manufacture, such as are usually or ordinarily marked, stamped, branded or labeled, and all packages containing such or other imported articles, shall, respectively, be plainly marked, stamped, branded or labeled in legible English words, so as to indicate the country of their origin. . .

CUSTOMS OFFICE CIRCULAR, DECEMBER 20, 1890

6. The prefix "from" placed before the name of the country of origin as, for instance, "from France," "from Germany," etc., is not essential, the law requiring simply the name of the country of origin to appear.

TRADEMARK ACT OF 1905 (FEBUARY 20, 1905)

Sec. 27. That no article of imported merchandise which shall copy or simulate the name of any domestic manufacture, or manufacturer or trader, or of any manufacturer or trader located in any foreign country . . . which shall copy or simulate a trademark registered in accordance with the provisions of this Act, or shall bear a name or mark calculated to induce the public to believe that the article is manufactured in the United States . . . shall be admitted to entry at any custom-house of the United States.

THE TARIFF ACT OF 1909, AUGUST 5, 1909

Chapter 6, Section 7 That all articles of foreign manufacture or production which are capable of being marked, stamped, branded or labeled, without injury, shall be marked, stamped, branded, or labeled in legible English words, in a conspicuous place that shall not be covered or obscured by any subsequent attachments or arrangements, so as to indicate the country of origin.

THE TARIFF ACT OF 1913, OCTOBER 3, 1913

Section 4, Subsection 1, Paragraph F That all articles of foreign manufacture or production which are capable of being marked, stamped, branded or labeled, without injury, shall be marked, stamped, branded or labeled in legible English words, in a conspicuous place that shall not be covered or obscured by any subsequent attachments or arrangements, so as to indicate the country of origin. Said marking, stamping, branding or labeling shall be as nearly indelible and permanent as the nature of the article will permit.

TREASURY DECISION T.D. 34740, AUGUST 1914
Marking of Japanese Imports

Sir: The department refers . . .to an inquiry from a customs broker at your port whether brushes manufactured in Japan and marked with the word "Nippon" would be considered as legally marked under . . .the tariff act of October 3, 1913. . . While it appears that the word "Nippon" is the Japanese name for Japan, it is so commonly employed in this country to designate Japan that it may now be considered as incorporated in our language with a well-established meaning. The department is therefore of the opinion that articles produced in Japan and marked with the word "Nippon" are legally marked under subsection 1 of paragraph F. . .

TREASURY DEPARTMENT T.D. 36989, FEBUARY 8, 1917
Marking Chinaware

Chinaware and porcelain not marked to indicate the country of origin at the time of importation may be released when marked by means of a gummed label or with a rubber stamp. . . Unless the merchandise is manufactured especially for the American trade, permanent marking is not required.

TREASURY DEPARTMENT T.D. 38643, MARCH 1, 1921

Marking of Japanese merchandise with the word "Nippon" not a compliance with the law-T.D.

Reference is made to the revisions of T.D. 34740 of August 31, 1914, and T.D. 37828 of December 9, 1918, by authority of which merchandise imported from Japan and marked with the name "Nippon" is admitted to entry as conforming, respectively, to (a) paragraph F, subsection 1, section IV, of the tariff act of 1913. . . . . .the department is constrained to the conclusion that "Nippon" is a Japanese word, the English equivalent of which is "Japan," and that the weight of authority does not support the earlier view that the word has become incorporated into the English language. . . .you are instructed that merchandise from Japan, the marking of which is governed by this provision of law, should not be released when bearing only the Japanese word "Nippon" to indicate Japan. You are further instructed, therefore, that imports from Japan. . .should not be permitted delivery unless marked with the English name of the country of origin, as well as the name of the maker or purchaser. T.D. 34740 and T.D. 37828 are, therefore hereby revoked, such provocation and the new practice herein outlined to become effective six months from the date hereof.

T.D. 40469 (NOVEMBER 4, 1924)

8. Articles in sets.—Salad sets of decorated earthenware imported from Czechoslovakia were marked on the largest piece only of each set to indicate the country of origin. It was held that such marking was insufficient and that each piece of the set must be marked under section 304 (a) of the tariff act.

T.D. 42995 (OCTOBER 10, 1928)

Bags containing cement from foreign countries should be plainly and conspicuously printed or stencilled with the name of the country of manufacture preceded by the words "Made in," under section 304 (a), tariff act of 1922.

TARIFF ACT OF 1930, SECTION 304 A, JUNE 17, 1930

(a) MANNER OF MARKING.—Every article imported into the United States, and its immediate container, and the package in which such article is imported, shall be marked, stamped, branded or labeled, in legible English words, in a conspicuous place, in such manner as to indicate the country of origin of such article, in accordance with such regulations as the Secretary of the Treasury may prescribe...

T.D. 44370 (NOVEMBER 17, 1930)

(5) Marking inducing purchasers to believe imported articles of American production.—Dental engine parts marked (stamped) with the name of the importer and the words "New York" as well as with the word "Germany" held to be prohibited entry under section 27 of the trade-mark law of February 20, 1905, and release of merchandise granted only upon the words "Made in" before the word "Germany."

(6) Sufficiency of marking—"Made in" when required.—It is not necessary that the words "Made in" shall precede the name "Switzerland" on merchandise imported from Switzerland, provided, of course, that any other words or descriptive matter appearing in conjunction therewith will not reasonably be apt to lead to confusion on the part of purchasers. . .If such confusion might reasonably exist, then the words "Made in" should precede the name of the country of origin.

TD 52162

Abstracts of unpublished decisions

MARKING

(2) "Made in Occupied Japan," "Made in Japan," "Japan," or "Occupied Japan" are acceptable markings to indicate the name of the country of origin under the marking provisions of the Tariff Act of 1930, as amended, of articles manufactured or produced in Japan. Bureau letter to collector of customs, Los Angeles, California, February 18, 1949. (363.22)

Bibliography

Anscombe, Isabelle & Charlotte Gere. *Arts & Crafts in Britain and America*. New York: Rizzoli International Publications, 1978.

Colcutt, Martin, Marius Jansen and Iseo Kumakura. *Cultural Atlas of Japan*. Oxford: Equinox, 1988.

Collier's Encyclopedia, Macmillan Educational Company, 1992.

Donahue, Lou Ann. *Noritake Collectibles*. Des Moines, Iowa: Wallace-Homestead Book Company, 1979.

Dorfles, Gillo. *Kitsch, The World of Bad Taste*. New York: Universe Books, 1969.

Encyclopedia Americana, Grolier, Inc., 1992.

Horn, Richard. *Fifties Style Then and Now*. New York: Beech Tree Books, William Morrow and Company, 1985.

Hull, John. *Art Deco, Decorative Designs of the Twenties and Thirties*. San Francisco: Troubador Press, 1975.

Klamkin, Marian. *Made in Occupied Japan, A Collector's Guide*. New York: Crown Publishers, 1976.

Klamkin, Marian. *The Collector's Book of Art Nouveau*. New York: Dodd, Mead & Company, 1971.

Klein, Dan. *All Color Book of Art Deco*. London: Octopus Books, 1974

Levy, Mervyn. *Liberty Style, The Classic Years: 1898-1910*. New York: Rizzoli International Publications, Inc., 1986.

"Made by Muriel Joséf George." *Antique Trader*. April 8, 1992.

Nelson, Glenn C. *Ceramics, A Potter's Handbook*. New York: Holt, Rinehart and Wilson, 1966.

Stern, Jane and Michael. *The Encylopedia of Bad Taste*. New York: Harper Collins Publishers, 1990.

U.S. Government. *Digest of Treasury Decisions*. All Volumes.

U.S. Government. *The Statutes at Large of the United States of America*. V.26, V.36, V.38, V.41, V.42, V.44, V.46, V.52, V.56.

United States Tariff Commission. *Pottery, Household Table and Kitchen Articles of Earthenware and of China, Porcelain, and Other Vitrified Wares; Report No. 102, Second Series*. Washington: United States Government Printing Office, 1936.

Washington State University Museum of Art. *Noritake Art Deco Porcelains, Collection of Howard Kottler*. 1982.

Van Patten, Joan F. *The Collector's Encylopedia of Nippon Porcelain*. Paducah, Kentucky: Collector Books, 1979.

Van Patten, Joan F. *The Collector's Encylopedia of Noritake*. Paducah, Kentucky: Collector Books, 1984, 1993.

✍ About the Author ✍

Carole Bess White has been a serious collector of Made in Japan since 1981. She fell in love with the pelican in Plate #94 ("the silliest, sorriest-looking thing I'd ever seen. . . I had to give it a home"), and that started a collection of about 600 pieces—so far. She is a Lifetime Member of Portland's Rain of Glass, a nonprofit society dedicated to collecting and studying nostalgia. Currently she is their Program/Publicity Chair, and she served as President for five years.

Carole has worked full time in newspaper entertainment advertising for more than 20 years.

For a number of years she was also a potter, producing wheel-thrown stoneware and raku vessels.

Research on Made in Japan is a major interest of Carole's, and she will continue her studies in this area.

Carole is also a 1930's movie fan, and a collector in many other categories including Depression Glass.

Although she writes regularly by vocation and avocation, this is her first book.

Les White, Ed.D., has spent many years working with photography and computers. At present he is the information technology coordinator for an area high school.

Les is NOT a collector and likens his life to "living in a museum," but says he won't complain as long as there is room for his computers!

The Whites reside in Portland, Oregon.

⚑ Index ⚑

COLLECTOR BOOKS
Informing Today's Collector

DOLLS, FIGURES & TEDDY BEARS

2079	**Barbie** Doll Fashion, Volume I, Eames	$24.95
3957	**Barbie** Exclusives, Rana	$18.95
4557	**Barbie**, The First 30 Years, Deutsch	$24.95
3810	**Chatty Cathy** Dolls, Lewis	$15.95
4559	Collectible **Action Figures**, 2nd Ed., Manos	$17.95
1529	Collector's Encyclopedia of **Barbie** Dolls, DeWein/Ashabraner	$19.95
2211	Collector's Encyclopedia of **Madame Alexander Dolls**, 1965-1990, Smith	$24.95
4863	Collector's Encyclopedia of **Vogue Dolls**, Stover/Izen	$29.95
4861	Collector's Guide to **Tammy**, Sabulis/Weglewski	$18.95
3967	Collector's Guide to **Trolls**, Peterson	$19.95
1799	**Effanbee Dolls**, Smith	$19.95
5253	Story of **Barbie**, 2nd Ed., Westenhouser	$24.95
1513	**Teddy Bears & Steiff** Animals, Mandel	$9.95
1817	**Teddy Bears & Steiff** Animals, 2nd Series, Mandel	$19.95
2084	**Teddy Bears, Annalee's & Steiff** Animals, 3rd Series, Mandel	$19.95
1808	Wonder of **Barbie**, Manos	$9.95
1430	World of **Barbie** Dolls, Manos	$9.95
4880	World of **Raggedy Ann Collectibles**, Avery	$24.95

TOYS, MARBLES & CHRISTMAS COLLECTIBLES

3427	**Advertising Character** Collectibles, Dotz	$17.95
2333	Antique & Collectible **Marbles**, 3rd Ed., Grist	$9.95
4934	**Breyer Animal** Collector's Guide, Identification and Values, Browell	$19.95
4976	**Christmas** Ornaments, Lights & Decorations, Johnson	$24.95
4737	**Christmas** Ornaments, Lights & Decorations, Vol. II, Johnson	$24.95
4739	**Christmas** Ornaments, Lights & Decorations, Vol. III, Johnson	$24.95
2338	Collector's Encyclopedia of **Disneyana**, Longest, Stern	$24.95
4958	Collector's Guide to **Battery Toys**, Hultzman	$19.95
5038	Collector's Guide to **Diecast Toys** & Scale Models, 2nd Ed., Johnson	$19.95
4566	Collector's Guide to **Tootsietoys**, 2nd Ed, Richter	$19.95
3436	**Grist's** Big Book of **Marbles**	$19.95
3970	**Grist's** Machine-Made & Contemporary **Marbles**, 2nd Ed.	$9.95
5267	**Matchbox** Toys, 3rd Ed., 1947 to 1998, Johnson	$19.95
4871	**McDonald's Collectibles**, Henriques/DuVall	$19.95
1540	**Modern Toys** 1930–1980, Baker	$19.95
3888	**Motorcycle** Toys, Antique & Contemporary, Gentry/Downs	$18.95
5168	**Schroeder's Collectible Toys**, Antique to Modern Price Guide, 5th Ed	$17.95
1886	**Stern's** Guide to **Disney** Collectibles	$14.95
2139	**Stern's** Guide to **Disney** Collectibles, 2nd Series	$14.95
3975	**Stern's** Guide to **Disney** Collectibles, 3rd Series	$18.95
2028	**Toys**, Antique & Collectible, Longest	$14.95

JEWELRY, HATPINS, WATCHES & PURSES

1712	Antique & Collectible **Thimbles** & Accessories, Mathis	$19.95
1748	Antique **Purses**, Revised Second Ed., Holiner	$19.95
1278	Art Nouveau & Art Deco **Jewelry**, Baker	$9.95
4850	Collectible **Costume Jewelry**, Simonds	$24.95
3875	Collecting Antique **Stickpins**, Kerins	$16.95
3722	Collector's Ency. of **Compacts, Carryalls & Face Powder Boxes**, Mueller	$24.95
4940	**Costume Jewelry**, A Practical Handbook & Value Guide, Rezazadeh	$24.95
1716	Fifty Years of Collectible **Fashion Jewelry**, 1925-1975, Baker	$19.95
1424	**Hatpins** & Hatpin Holders, Baker	$9.95
1181	100 Years of Collectible **Jewelry**, 1850-1950, Baker	$9.95
2348	20th Century Fashionable Plastic **Jewelry**, Baker	$19.95
3830	Vintage **Vanity Bags & Purses**, Gerson	$24.95

FURNITURE

1457	American **Oak** Furniture, McNerney	$9.95
3716	American **Oak** Furniture, Book II, McNerney	$12.95
1118	Antique **Oak** Furniture, Hill	$7.95
2132	Collector's Encyclopedia of **American** Furniture, Vol. I, Swedberg	$24.95
2271	Collector's Encyclopedia of **American** Furniture, Vol. II, Swedberg	$24.95
3720	Collector's Encyclopedia of **American** Furniture, Vol. III, Swedberg	$24.95
1755	Furniture of the **Depression Era**, Swedberg	$19.95
3906	**Heywood-Wakefield** Modern Furniture, Rouland	$18.95
1885	**Victorian** Furniture, Our American Heritage, McNerney	$9.95
3829	**Victorian** Furniture, Our American Heritage, Book II, McNerney	$9.95

INDIANS, GUNS, KNIVES, TOOLS, PRIMITIVES

1868	Antique **Tools**, Our American Heritage, McNerney	$9.95
1426	**Arrowheads** & Projectile Points, Hothem	$7.95
2279	**Indian** Artifacts of the Midwest, Hothem	$14.95
3885	**Indian** Artifacts of the Midwest, Book II, Hothem	$16.95
5162	**Modern Guns**, Identification & Values, 12th Ed., Quertermous	$12.95
2164	**Primitives**, Our American Heritage, McNerney	$9.95
1759	**Primitives**, Our American Heritage, Series II, McNerney	$14.95
4730	Standard **Knife** Collector's Guide, 3rd Ed., Ritchie & Stewart	$12.95 .

PAPER COLLECTIBLES & BOOKS

4633	**Big Little Books**, A Collector's Reference & Value Guide, Jacobs	$18.95
4710	Collector's Guide to **Children's Books**, 1850 to 1950, Jones	$18.95
1441	Collector's Guide to **Post Cards**, Wood	$9.95
2081	Guide to Collecting **Cookbooks**, Allen	$14.95
2080	Price Guide to **Cookbooks** & Recipe Leaflets, Dickinson	$9.95
3973	**Sheet Music** Reference & Price Guide, 2nd Ed., Pafik & Guiheen	$19.95
4654	**Victorian Trade Cards**, Historical Reference & Value Guide, Cheadle	$19.95
4733	**Whitman Juvenile Books**, Brown	$17.95

OTHER COLLECTIBLES

2269	Antique **Brass & Copper** Collectibles, Gaston	$16.95
1880	Antique **Iron**, McNerney	$9.95
3872	Antique **Tins**, Dodge	$24.95
1128	**Bottle** Pricing Guide, 3rd Ed., Cleveland	$7.95
3718	Collectible **Aluminum**, Grist	$16.95
4560	Collectible **Cats**, An Identification & Value Guide, Book II, Fyke	$19.95
4852	Collectible **Compact Disc** Price Guide 2, Cooper	$17.95
2018	Collector's Encyclopedia of **Granite Ware**, Greguire	$24.95
3430	Collector's Encyclopedia of **Granite Ware**, Book II, Greguire	$24.95
4705	Collector's Guide to Antique **Radios**, 4th Ed., Bunis	$18.95
4933	Collector's Guide to **Bookends**, Identification & Values, Kuritzky	$19.95
3880	Collector's Guide to **Cigarette Lighters**, Flanagan	$17.95
4887	Collector's Guide to **Creek Chub Lures** & Collectibles, Smith	$24.95
3966	Collector's Guide to **Inkwells**, Identification & Values, Badders	$18.95
3881	Collector's Guide to **Novelty Radios**, Bunis/Breed	$18.95
4652	Collector's Guide to **Transistor Radios**, 2nd Ed., Bunis	$16.95
4864	Collector's Guide to **Wallace Nutting Pictures**, Ivankovich	$18.95
1629	**Doorstops**, Identification & Values, Bertoia	$9.95
3968	**Fishing Lure** Collectibles, Murphy/Edmisten	$24.95
5259	**Flea Market Trader**, 12th Ed., Huxford	$9.95
4945	**G-Men and FBI Toys**, Whitworth	$18.95
3819	**General Store** Collectibles, Wilson	$24.95
2216	**Kitchen Antiques**, 1790–1940, McNerney	$14.95
4950	The **Lone Ranger**, Collector's Reference & Value Guide, Felbinger	$18.95
2026	**Railroad** Collectibles, 4th Ed., Baker	$14.95
1632	**Salt & Pepper Shakers**, Guarnaccia	$9.95
1888	**Salt & Pepper Shakers** II, Guarnaccia	$14.95
2220	**Salt & Pepper Shakers** III, Guarnaccia	$14.95
3443	**Salt & Pepper Shakers** IV, Guarnaccia	$18.95
2096	**Silverplated Flatware**, Revised 4th Edition, Hagan	$14.95
1922	Standard **Old Bottle** Price Guide, Sellari	$14.95
3892	**Toy & Miniature Sewing Machines**, Thomas	$18.95
5144	Value Guide to **Advertising Memorabilia**, 2nd Ed., Summers	$19.95
3977	Value Guide to **Gas Station** Memorabilia, Summers	$24.95
4877	Vintage **Bar Ware**, Visakay	$24.95
4935	The **W.F. Cody Buffalo Bill** Collector's Guide with Values, Wojtowicz	$24.95
5281	**Wanted to Buy**, 7th Edition	$9.95

GLASSWARE & POTTERY

4929	**American Art Pottery**, 1880 – 1950, Sigafoose	$24.95
4938	Collector's Encyclopedia of **Depression Glass**, 13th Ed., Florence	$19.95
5040	Collector's Encyclopedia of **Fiesta**, 8th Ed., Huxford	$19.95
4946	Collector's Encyclopedia of **Howard Pierce Porcelain**, Dommel	$24.95
1358	Collector's Encyclopedia of **McCoy Pottery**, Huxford	$19.95
2339	Collector's Guide to **Shawnee Pottery**, Vanderbilt	$19.95
1523	Colors in **Cambridge Glass**, National Cambridge Society	$19.95
3725	**Fostoria**, Pressed, Blown & Hand Molded Shapes, Kerr	$24.95
4726	**Red Wing Art Pottery**, 1920s – 1960s, Dollen	$19.95